SO-EDI-312

PAIUTE, PROSPECTOR, PIONEER

PAIUTE, PROSPECTOR, PIONEER

PAIUTE, PROSPECTOR, PIONEER

The Bodie-Mono Lake Area in the
Nineteenth Century

THOMAS C. FLETCHER

Community Printing & Publishing
Bishop, California

COMMUNITY PRINTING & PUBLISHING
187 West Line Street, Suite B
Bishop, California 93514

Front cover illustration: John Muir visiting a Kuzedika camp, north-west shore of Mono Lake, about 1900. Photo by C. Hart Merriam. Courtesy of the Bancroft Library.

Back cover illustration: Old-growth Jeffrey pine logs at wood landing, Mono Mills, date unknown. Courtesy of Mono Lake Committee Research Library.

To Barbara Lee Maxwell Fletcher

CONTENTS

FIGURES

ILLUSTRATIONS

Acknowledgments

I owe thanks to many people who devoted their time, expertise and knowledge to the completion of this book. I am extremely grateful to my wife, Susan Fletcher, for her able assistance in field and library research and her unstinting editorial help through numerous drafts; to David and Sally Gaines of Artemisia Press for enthusiastically taking on this project, locating illustrations and historic photographs, and suggesting many improvements to the text; to Adrienne Morgan, cartographer of the Geography Department at the University of California at Berkeley, for drawing the original maps; and to Scott Stine for many valuable suggestions and interest. In addition I would like to thank the following people for their assistance; by locating scarce sources of information, suggesting lines of inquiry and providing me with contacts among their friends and peers, they made major contributions: Bob Hawley of Ross Valley Book Company in Albany, California; Robert B. Matchette, Navy and Old Army Branch, Military Archives Division, National Archives and Records Service, Washington, D.C.; Rich Weaver, Forest Archaeologist, Inyo National Forest, Bishop, California; David Herbst, Entomology Department, Oregon State University, Corvallis, Oregon; George Stammerjohan, California Department of Parks and Recreation, Sacramento, California; Eric Levy, Bishop Resource Area Archaeologist, Bureau of Land Management, Bishop, California; Mary Vocelka, Librarian, Yosemite Research Library, and Craig Bates, Assistant Curator, Yosemite Museum, Yosemite National Park, California.

Introduction

For over one hundred years the marked contrasts and complexities of the Mono Basin landscape—its huge island-dotted and drainless lake, its volcanic domes and glacial moraines nestled together at the base of the Sierra Nevada's spectacular eastern wall—have fascinated observers of the West, including Mark Twain, John Muir and a host of others. The extraordinary nature of these landforms was brilliantly conveyed in Israel C. Russell's classic *Quaternary History of Mono Valley, California* (1889), the first detailed monograph on the geologic history of any part of eastern California or the Sierra Nevada. Since Russell's pioneering work, many studies have been published on the geology and glacial history of the Mono Basin and on the ecology of Mono Lake. In contrast the historical geography of the basin—the story of its discovery by westward-moving Americans, early settlement and economic development in the nineteenth century—has been largely ignored.

Those who have written about the Mono Basin's early history, e.g. W. A. Chalfant, Margaret Calhoun, Ella Cain and Frank Wedertz, have either been descendants of the pioneers themselves, or have depended heavily on the accounts of such descendants. In general they have passed on an inherited tradition, a legacy of the pioneering days that abounds in myths and exaggeration, with few facts to act as ballast. I have undertaken the present study to fill this gap, and to tip the balance from fancy to fact.

The nineteenth century was an era of intense change and development in the Mono Basin, spanning the time from when whites first set foot in the area to the coming of railroads, steamboats, electricity and the city of Los Angeles. Because the Mono Basin lay slightly off the paths beaten to California by the trappers and early pioneers, it was not entered by whites until 1852. But it was the first area east of the Sierran crest and south of Lake Tahoe to boast a town: Monoville. This mining village sprang up suddenly in 1859, and its boom marked the beginning of an era of intensive exploitation of the basin's minerals, soils, timber and rangeland which lasted nearly to the end of the century. Throughout this period insularity characterized basin life. Society was to a large extent self-sufficient, local in focus, almost hermetic. After the turn of the century, in contrast, the outside world (especially Los Angeles) profoundly influenced the basin and transformed the self-sufficient farming, ranching and mining economy into one dependent on tourism and governmental services. In this study, however, I concentrate upon the earlier, isolated period when the people who exploited the basin's resources lived there and used them there, returning in substantial measure the fruits of their labors to the basin itself.

My account is divided into four chapters. As a preparation for later discussions, Chapter 1 summarizes salient physical and vegetational features of the landscape and briefly describes the traditional food-procurement practices and trade relations of the native human inhabitants, the Kuzedika Paiute.

Chapter 2 takes up the subject of the discovery of Mono Lake by white men. Two famous trappers and explorers, Jedediah Smith and Joseph Walker, have been repeatedly and dubiously cited by local historians as the first to see the lake, while its real discoverer, Lt. Tredwell Moore of the Second Infantry, has languished in obscurity. I present here for the first time three previously unknown letters written by Moore to his superiors while on his expedition of discovery in 1852; they had lain buried in the vast repository of military correspondence at the National Archives in Washington D.C. These letters shed new light on the concluding action of the Mariposa Indian War of 1851-52 and correct inaccuracies in our knowledge of Moore's explorations through the High Sierra of today's Yosemite National Park.

Less than three years after Moore's discovery of Mono Lake, Alexis W. von Schmidt was hired by the Surveyor General of the United States to survey the region—the first part of California east of the Sierra Nevada to be surveyed. The task required four expeditions on the part of von Schmidt, whose unpublished journals, plats, sketch maps and notes provide us with important knowledge of physical conditions in Mono Basin at that time.

Chapter 3 examines the beginnings of economic development in the Mono region: the first mining activities and the sudden birth of Monoville; the establishment of the first agricultural settlements around Mono Lake in the 1850s and 1860s; and the effects of these developments on the Kuzedika Paiute. Their lands usurped, the Kuzedika found their age-old ways of life increasingly difficult to maintain and began to trade with, work for and depend upon the white settlers and their economy.

The bulk of the book, Chapter 4, chronicles the rise of the mining town of Bodie, beginning in 1877, and its stimulating effect upon mining, lumbering and agriculture in Mono Basin. Just as the discovery of Mono Lake has been the subject of fable and exaggeration, so too has been the lively but relatively brief history of this famous mining town. Although the boom period at Bodie was short, it lasted long enough to greatly affect the basin's natural landscape. Waves of new settlers founded new towns—Lundy, Wasson, Bennettville, Mono Mills—opened up scores of new mines, established farms and ranches all around Mono Lake, and built sawmills in the principal timber stands to supply the lumber for the intense developments. Contemporary newspapers, hitherto largely overlooked, have provided a rich source of original information on this period—especially the *Homer Mining Index*, first published at Lundy in 1880.

I have tried to present a clearly focused and integrated picture of the Mono Basin landscape through a 75-year period of intense change. In so doing, I have attempted to identify the inaccuracies and unfounded assertions which litter popular histories. Finally I have assembled, for the first time, excerpts from the most vivid and informative contemporary descriptions and reports.

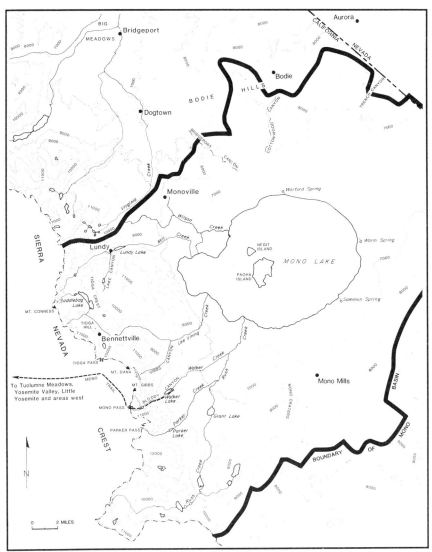

Figure 1. *Mono Basin place names and boundary.*

Chapter 1

THE BACKGROUND

The Physical Setting

Mono Basin is located immediately east of Yosemite National Park, approximately 180 miles east of San Francisco and 350 miles north of Los Angeles. The name "Mono Basin" designates the drainage basin of Mono Lake, that is, the 700 square mile area from which the lake receives surface runoff and groundwater inflows. It includes not only the tectonically depressed lowland in which Mono Lake lies, but also those portions of the surrounding hills and mountains—the Sierra Nevada, Anchorite and Bodie Hills, and Mono Craters—which slope toward the lake. Over 90 percent of the basin lies in California; its easternmost corner extends into Nevada (Figure 1).

Under natural conditions the Mono Basin was of the "closed" or "interior" type, meaning that Mono Lake, which received all the runoff from the major streams, had no outlet. Since 1940, however, the city of Los Angeles has diverted much of the inflow, creating an artificial outlet and causing a steady decline of the lake's surface level. Elevations within the basin range from 6,372 feet at the surface of Mono Lake (in 1982) to 13,053 feet at Mt Dana's summit, a difference of almost 7,000 feet.

Most of Mono Basin lies in the strong rain-shadow of the Sierra Nevada, which acts as a barrier to moisture-laden air from the Pacific Ocean. Average annual precipitation declines rapidly from west to east across the basin. The yearly average at Ellery Lake near the Sierran crest is 25.6 inches, but at the west shore of Mono Lake, only five miles to the east, it is about 13 inches. East of Mono Lake precipitation is very low, between five and ten inches annually.[1] About 90 percent of the annual precipitation falls in winter as snow.[2] In addition to the low average totals, precipitation is also highly variable, with extremely wet or dry years a common occurrence.

The basin's pronounced vertical relief and climatic gradients cause strong zonation of floral associations. The eastern base of the Sierra Nevada marks the boundary between two major floristic provinces, the Sierran and Nevadan.[3] The Sierran province consists of montane vegetation types, represented in Mono Basin by the Alpine Fell-field, Subalpine Forest and Mixed Coniferous Forest communities. The Nevadan province is characterized by high-desert associations, expressed here by the Pinyon-Juniper Woodland and Sagebrush Scrub communities.

The Sagebrush Scrub is by far the most extensive plant community, occupying most of the gentler slopes and flat areas below 7,000 feet. In arid parts of the basin north and east of Mono Lake the sagebrush reaches higher elevations, up to 10,000 feet in the Bodie Hills. Big sagebrush (*Artemisia tridentata*) is usually the dominant species, although other shrubs are well-represented, including rabbitbrush (*Chrysothamnus nauseosus*), desert peach (*Prunus andersonii*) and bitterbrush (*Purshia tridentata*), the last a valuable browse for deer and livestock. Under pristine conditions the spaces between the shrubs were filled with a variety of perennial grasses, especially giant wildrye (*Elymus cinereus*) and Indian ricegrass (*Oryzopsis hymenoides*).

Pinyon-Juniper Woodland clothes slopes above the floor of the basin between 7,000 and 8,000 feet in elevation. Dominated by two coniferous species, pinyon (or nut) pine (*Pinus monophylla*) and Utah juniper (*Juniperus osteosperma*), the woodland contains an understory of shrubs, primarily sagebrush, rabbitbrush and bitterbrush; grasses are sparse. In Mono Basin these two trees tend to form separate bands, pinyon above and juniper below, across the south flank of the Bodie Hills from Bridgeport Canyon east to the Nevada state line.[4] On the eastern slope of the Sierra, the pinyon occurs alone in patches above the sagebrush; Utah juniper is absent.

Mixed Coniferous Forest occupies a band along the eastern flank of the Sierra Nevada between 7,500 and 9,500 feet. Tree species in this community include lodgepole pine (*Pinus contorta* var. *murrayana*), Jeffrey pine (*Pinus Jeffreyi*), western white pine (*Pinus monticola*), red fir (*Abies magnifica*) and white fir (*Abies concolor*).

A large, pure stand of Jeffrey pine covers a broad area south of Mono Lake, where the climate is locally more moist than at similar elevations elsewhere in the basin. The wetter climate is due to a low gap in the Sierran crest near the headwaters of the middle fork of the San Joaquin River between Mammoth and Agnew passes. The gap allows more winter precipitation to penetrate into the basin. The forest is composed of almost pure stands of Jeffrey pine, with an understory of shrubs, herbs and grasses.[5]

Finally, riparian vegetation occupies the streambanks descending from the Sierra Nevada and Bodie Hills, dominated by willows (*Salix*), cottonwood and aspen (*Populus*). Extensive meadows occur along the lower reaches of streams, and smaller meadows are maintained by springs and seeps at scattered locations around Mono Lake, in the Bodie Hills and southeast of the Mono Craters.

The Kuzedika Paiute

For hundreds of years prior to the entry of the first Europeans, Mono Basin was the home of a group of Northern Paiute Indians who called themselves the Kuzedika, or "Fly-larvae Eaters," after a distinctive element of their diet.[6] Archaeological evidence, including petroglyphs and stone points and blades, indicate that the Kuzedika Paiute were not the first human inhabitants of the basin, but were the latest in a series of occupying peoples, the first of whom entered at least 5,500 years ago.[7]

The Kuzedika were hunters and gatherers who relied upon a great diversity of plant and animal foods. They moved from place to place within and beyond the basin to take advantage of seasonal grass seeds, roots, tubers, pinenuts, large and small game, and insects. Although they could depend upon a wide variety of foods, they had to endure occasional years of scarcity and famine. Their population was restricted to the number that could be supported in the worst years, possibly not more than 200.[8]

Their winter staple was the nut of the pinyon pine, but the crop was not reliable, sometimes failing completely. When food stores were low, the Kuzedika families sought refuge with relatives to the east and south, or with the Miwok of

Yosemite Valley.[9] Gentle winters were spent on the east shore or near the pinenut groves north of the lake.[10]

During the spring and early summer, the Kuzedika lived along the streams draining the Sierra Nevada. After a winter diet of pinenut mush and an occasional rodent or rabbit, they welcomed fresh vegetables such as wild onions and lily bulbs, and the fresh meat supplied in quantity by mule deer returning to the Sierra from their winter range to the east. In the meadows and meadow-edges and in favored spots within the sagebrush, the Kuzedika collected the seeds of a variety of bunchgrasses—giant wildrye, Indian ricegrass, and desert needlegrass (*Stipa speciosa*)—throughout the late spring and summer.

Summer was the time of the Kuzedika's most intense and varied activity. Groups of men climbed high into the Sierra in search of deer and bighorn sheep, and packed the kill down to the summer camps. The Kuzedika also collected a wide variety of berries and fruits, especially desert peach, elderberries (*Sambucus mexicana*), and buffalo berries (*Shepherdia argentea*).[11]

The two most important summer foods, however, were insects. Late each summer the Kuzedika moved to the shores of the lake, especially the north shore, to collect and dry *kutsavi*, the larvae of a brine fly (*Ephydra hians*).[12] Other Paiute groups and Washo Indians from the north often joined them in this harvest.[13] In alternate years, beginning in early July, they collected large quantities of the caterpillars of a moth, *Coloradia pandora*, in the Jeffrey pine forest south of Mono Lake.[14] Other insect foods included ant eggs, crickets and the larvae of wasps and bees.[15]

In late summer and early fall the Kuzedika held rabbit drives around the lake flats. The drives required the participation of many people, some to hold the long nets into which the rabbits were driven, others to light fires in the sagebrush and force the rabbits into the nets.[16] With the coming of fall the pinenut harvest began again, and the yearly cycle was completed.

Thus, through the year, the Kuzedika moved in an established sequence from one favored locality to another according to the availability of food. Their routes of travel were well-defined; the basin was honeycombed with trails linking their seasonal camp sites.[17]

The Kuzedika also travelled far beyond the confines of the Mono Lake watershed; their trade and social relations with neighboring tribes was extensive. Every summer after the passes were sufficiently free of snow, the Kuzedika made hurried trips from Mono Lake to Yosemite Valley and other summer camps of the Central Miwok, carrying such trade goods as pinenuts, dried caterpillars, *kutsavi*, baskets, red and white paints, salt, obsidian, pumice,

Kuzedika wikiups on the east shore of Mono Lake. Photo, C. Hart Merriam, circa 1900. Courtesy, the Bancroft Library.

rabbit-skin blankets and sinew-backed bows.[18] In return the Kuzedika sought acorns, manzanita berries, shell beads, bear skins, arrows, baskets and black and yellow paints.[19] The trade with the Miwok was a two-way affair; sometimes the Kuzedika and sometimes the Miwok made the trade journey. As mentioned above, the Kuzedika occasionally wintered with the Miwok in Yosemite Valley. Relations between the two groups were close, and marriage between them common.[20] The Kuzedika also traded and intermarried with other Paiute groups from Bridgeport Basin, Walker Lake, Soda Springs Valley and especially Owens Valley.

The Kuzedika's primary route to and from Yosemite Valley and environs was the "Mono Trail" (named in the late 1850s by miners using it to enter Mono Basin). From Mono Lake the trail passed up Bloody Canyon, over Mono Pass and along the Dana Fork of the Tuolumne River to Tuolumne Meadows, where it forked. The north branch went west, crossing the headwaters of Cathedral Creek to Tenaya Lake and continuing along the divide between the Merced and Tuolumne rivers through Porcupine, Tamarack and Crane flats and on to Crockers (at the present Big Oak Flat entrance station to Yosemite National Park). From Porcupine Flat a side-trail branched off to the south to enter

Yosemite Valley via Indian Canyon; this trail was the principal route used by the Yosemite Miwok to reach the highlands above the valley.

The other main branch of the Mono Trail left Tuolumne Meadows via Cathedral Pass, crossed Long Meadow and entered Little Yosemite Valley about one mile above Nevada Fall (today's Sunrise section of the John Muir Trail). Little Yosemite Valley was a favorite summer deer-hunting ground of the Kuzedika.[21] The trail continued to the southeast up Panorama Cliff, crossed upper Illilouette Creek, Mono and Westfall meadows, and passed through Wawona toward present Mariposa.

All the branches of the Mono Trail were clearly marked and much used by both the east- and west-slope Indians. When whites began to penetrate the region, these trails became the principal routes of travel. They remain heavily used even today; the Tioga Road (Highway 120) follows the north branch from the Big Oak Flat park entrance to near Tioga Pass.

Kuzedika Paiute woman and child in Yosemite Valley, circa 1900. Photograph by J.T. Boysen. Courtesy Yosemite National Park Research Library.

Chapter 2

EARLIEST EXPLORATIONS, 1827-1857

Legendary Discoverers:
Jedediah Smith and Joseph Walker

Though they named the range and some of the rivers descending its western flank, the Spaniards and Mexicans of early California never crossed the high mountains east of the Central Valley. Spanish traders and adventurers from New Mexico moved into the Utah Country, but never came near the Sierra Nevada from the east. Thus it was left to Americans to traverse the range for the first time.

The famous trapper and explorer Jedediah Smith made the pioneer crossing, not from east to west as one might expect, but in the reverse direction. Late in 1826 Smith led a party of trappers into California, following the course of the Inconstant River (the Mojave) west across the desert. The purpose of the expedition was to explore north along the west coast and to assess the area's potential as a source of furs for market. By May, 1827, Smith and his men had advanced well north into the Central Valley, but were desperately low in provisions. Smith decided to leave most of his men behind and make a quick journey to the Bear River rendezvous north of Great Salt Lake for replenishment. Taking two companions, Smith crossed the Sierra Nevada from west to east in late spring, 1827, the first known crossing by non-Indians.

Smith's exact route over the Sierra has been the subject of much debate. To this day, in popular histories of Mono and Inyo counties, we read that Smith, en route to Salt Lake, entered the Mono Basin and discovered gold on the shores of Mono Lake. According to Francis Farquhar, the foremost historian of the Sierra Nevada, this tale was a "required subject" among early pioneers to California.[1] Eminent nineteenth-century historians of the West, including Hubert Howe Bancroft and Myron Angel, relied too heavily on the recollections of these old-timers and lent support to this legend.

In his *History of California*, Bancroft attempted to reconstruct Smith's route but was finally unable to choose between two possibilities he deemed equally likely: a crossing of the Sierra at Donner Pass (the most northerly possible route) and one at Walker Pass (the most southerly).[2] In support of the Walker Pass hypothesis, Bancroft cited a recollection of one early pioneer, Thomas Sprague, who suggested that Smith reached Mono Lake and found gold:

> He crossed the mountains near what is now known as Walker's Pass, and skirted the eastern slope of the mountains to near what is now known as Mono Lake, when he steered an east by north course for Salt Lake. On this portion of his route he found placer gold in quantities, and brought much of it with him to the encampment on Green River.[3]

Bancroft also cited a second pioneer account bearing on Smith's "visit" to Mono Lake, which had been published in Angel's *History of Nevada*.[4]

> The only information in our possession in regard to the direction taken by Smith on his return trip across the country is contained in the following extract from a letter to us upon that subject from Captain Robert Lyon, of San Buenaventura, California: "...His, Smith's notes [the whereabouts of which are now unknown] mention the discovery of Mono Lake (or dead sea) in his return trip in 1825 [this, of course, was 1827]...Rocky Mountain Jack, or Uncle Jack, as he was called, and Bill Reed both spent the summer of 1860 at Mono, and were well known at that time, and both of these old trappers declared they were with Smith in 1825, and that they spent a week prospecting and picking up gold in these foot-hills in 1825...Bill Byrnes, well known in Carson City, always claimed that Jed Smith discovered the Mono mines in 1825 although he (Byrnes) was not of the party."[5]

Bancroft's and Angel's sources of information on Smith's route are suspect, and can be, as Farquhar says, "dismissed from the historical record."[6] Twentieth-century research, moreover, has solved the mystery of Smith's crossing. In 1934 Maurice Sullivan discovered a transcript of Smith's lost diary for 1827, which clearly indicates that he left his men on the north bank of the Stanislaus River and crossed the range a short distance north of Ebbett's Pass, well to the north of Mono Basin.[7]

Unfortunately, Bancroft's erroneous "evidence" has not been completely put to rest. The legend of Smith's visit to Mono Lake lives on in such popular histories of Mono and Inyo counties as Chalfant's *The Story of Inyo* (latest printing 1975) and Wedertz's *Mono Diggings* (1978).

Similar confusion persists with regard to the 1833 explorations of Joseph Reddeford Walker; the uncertainties may never be resolved. In this case historians must rely on the personal reminiscences of one of Walker's companions on the trip, his clerk, Zenas Leonard. The *Narrative of the Adventures of Zenas Leonard* was published in 1839, five years after Leonard's return to Pennsylvania from the West; it contains a lengthy and detailed account of the Walker expedition to California in 1833. They were a large party of more than 70 well-armed men, intent upon opening up a new route to the Pacific. Their journey was extremely important from a geographical standpoint, for it included the first crossing of the Sierra Nevada by white men from east to west, the discovery of Yosemite Valley, and the first sighting of big tree (*Sequoiadendron*) groves.

Some authors have suggested, based on passages in Leonard's memoir, that Walker's party also discovered Mono Lake. The pertinent sections contain descriptions of Indians and their activities, and of certain physical features associated with large lakes. Interpretations of these passages, however, must take into consideration the overall reliability of the narrative as a whole, and the topographical and chronological contexts of each description.

When assessing Leonard's reliability it is important to keep in mind that he was writing mostly from memory about a trip he had taken five years earlier. The bulk of his own notes had been stolen although, writes his original publisher, he had Walker's journal at his disposal—a dubious claim. He was describing unnamed and unmapped places that, because they resembled each other, could easily have become confused in his mind. Given these factors, the *Narrative* undoubtedly contains inaccuracies. Moreover, Leonard's descriptions of terrain are often hopelessly vague, and his chronology muddled or implausible. Nevertheless, his account is not without value, and makes the most sense if we infer that the party, after leaving the Carson Lakes, travelled southwest into the Sierra Nevada via the Walker River, bypassing Mono Lake completely.

Joseph Reddeford Walker. Courtesy, the Bancroft Library.

Historians agree that the Walker party left the Green River rendezvous on July 24, 1833, and journeyed west across the Great Salt Lake basin and along the Humboldt River to its end at Humboldt Lake, where, according to Leonard, the party arrived on September 4 (Figure 2, page 16).[8] This date is probably in error, because he gives the same date for the party's arrival at the west shore of Great Salt Lake weeks earlier. John Ewers suggests this second September 4 is a misprint, and that Leonard intended October 4. According to Leonard, the party left the Humboldt Lake area on October 10, still early enough to avoid winter conditions in the Sierra Nevada. From Humboldt Lake they moved south along the more-or-less continuous system of North and South Carson lakes. Their stock were half-starved after crossing the desert and were allowed to fatten on the abundant grass growing around the lakes.

Despite a deadly encounter with a large band of Northern Paiute, in which Walker's men killed 39, Leonard seems to have had ample opportunity to observe the Indians living along the lake shores. He describes Paiute food-procurement practices in considerable detail, one of which, the collection of *kutsavi*, has led some to the erroneous conclusion that the party was at Mono Lake:[9]

These lakes are all joined together by means of the river which passes from one to another, until it reaches the largest, which has no outlet. The water in this lake becomes stagnant and very disagreeable—its surface being covered with a green substance, similar to a stagnant frog pond. In warm weather there is a fly, about the size and similar to a grain of wheat, on this lake, in great numbers. When the wind rolls the waters onto the shore, these flies are left on the beach—the female Indians then carefully gather them into baskets made of willow branches, and lay them exposed to the sun until they become perfectly dry, when they are laid away for winter provender. These flies, together with grass seed, and a few rabbits, is [sic] their principal food during the winter season.[10]

There are a number of reasons why this lake was undoubtedly not Mono. In the *Narrative*, the above quoted passage is immediately preceded by a detailed description of the spearing of frogs and fish in lakes nearby; the Kuzedika of Mono Lake had no such opportunities. Furthermore, Mono Lake is not the largest of a connected series of similar lakes; the topographical context suggests one of the Carson Lakes. Finally, if it is assumed that the Walker party was at Mono Lake when the observation of *kutsavi* collection was made, it becomes impossible to make sense of the descriptions of the country traversed on the remainder of the journey into California.

It is quite possible, however, that the Paiute were harvesting brine fly larvae somewhere in the Carson Desert, as the *Narrative* clearly implies. Brine flies breed in considerable numbers in the Soda Lakes, about halfway between North and South Carson lakes. The larvae from the Soda Lakes were gathered by Northern Paiute bands.[11] The water bodies of Carson Desert vary greatly in size from year to year under natural conditions, depending upon precipitation; Leonard's "largest" lake may have been an ephemeral one, or a permanent lake temporarily enlarged. In sum, it is far more likely that Leonard's observations were made in the Carson Desert than in Mono Basin.

It is even possible, given the inaccuracies which could have crept into the *Narrative* due to the passage of five years before its writing, that the observation of *kutsavi-* harvesting was made at Owens Lake at the south end of Owens

Valley. *Kutsavi* occurred there in an abundance comparable to Mono Lake's.[12] Although he does not mention it, Leonard must have passed Owens Lake with Walker on their return from California in 1834. In these descriptions, then, he may have been projecting a scene he saw on his return east onto the westward journey of the previous year.

Leonard's *Narrative* continues:

> On the 10th of October we left these Indians and built rafts out of rushes to convey us across the river, when we left the lakes and continued our course in the direction of a large mountain, which was in sight, and which we could see was covered with snow on the summit. In the evening we encamped on the margin of a large lake formed by a river which heads in this mountain. This lake, likewise, has no outlet for the water, except that which sinks in the ground. The water in the lake is similar to lie, and tastes much like pearlash. If this river was in the vicinity of some city, it would be of inestimable value, as it is admirably calculated to wash clothes without soap, and no doubt could be appropriated to many valuable uses. There is also a great quantity of pumice stone floating on the surface of the water, and the shore is covered with them. The next day we traveled up this river towards the mountain, where we encamped for the night. This mountain is very high, as the snow extends down the side nearly halfway—the mountain runs north and south.[13]

This passage seems to confirm the fact that the party had indeed arrived at Mono Lake. The description of the lake water ("tastes much like pearlash") is remarkably similar to later appraisals of Mono Lake's alkaline water (for example, Mark Twain's facetious account in *Roughing It*). The presence of "pumice stone" also suggests Mono Lake; pumice blocks ejected from its volcanic islets or from Panum Crater litter its shore.

Again, however, Leonard's description must be approached critically. First, the topographical and chronological contexts do not support the case for arrival at Mono Lake. Leonard has the party arriving on October 11, but it would have been impossible for them to cover the distance from South Carson Lake to Mono Lake (some 80 miles as the crow flies) in one day's march. Nor is Mono Lake in a direct line of travel to the "large mountain," that is, the Sierra Nevada; reaching it would require a considerable detour south, either over or around intervening hills and mountains, none of which is even hinted at by Leonard. Such a route would have little appeal to a large party with many stock animals already weakened by the crossing of Utah and Nevada.

In contrast, both the Walker and Carson rivers offered easy and attractive routes which directly approach the Sierra Nevada. Indeed, Leonard expressly says that the party travelled "up this river towards the mountain." It is unlikely that any of the small streams flowing into Mono Lake would have been singled out as a river by Leonard. The question then becomes, which river did the Walker party follow, the Carson or the Walker?

The most likely location for that night's camp is at the north end of Walker Lake, which Leonard could have reached in one day's journey from the Carson Desert. The "river... of inestimable value" was probably the Walker River, which does indeed head in the "large mountain." Walker Lake water, while not as alkaline as that of Mono Lake, was certainly noticeably strong to the taste even prior to water diversions in the late nineteenth century.[14] And, once again, it is possible that the observation of strongly alkaline water was in fact made at Owens Lake on the return journey in 1834, but projected, by a slip of memory, onto the events of the journey west.

This interpretation has the added advantage of allowing sense to be made of subsequent topographical details. It took the party six days, Leonard says, to reach the crest of the Sierra Nevada from the lake, much of that time spent in searching for a route up the eastern flank of the range. Had they already reached Mono Lake, the ascent up the easily visible Bloody Canyon-Mono Pass route could have been made in one day, along the clearly demarcated trail used by the Kuzedika.

The sole element of Leonard's account which fits Mono Lake and no other is the floating pumice. In the face of the preponderance of evidence suggesting the unlikelihood of such an arrival, however, it is doubtful that the mention of pumice is sufficient in itself to uphold a claim for the Walker party's discovery of Mono Lake. In addition, while pumice does sit on the lake shore, it actually floats in the lake water infrequently, so that unlikelihoods compound. Rarely, small quantities are swept into the lake by high stream flows in Lee Vining and Rush creeks after unusually heavy storms in the Sierra Nevada; such heavy storms would be virtually confined to the winter and spring months. Larger quantities might be set adrift from the lake and island margins by a sudden rise in lake level, but such a rise would not occur in early fall, the low-flow period for tributary streams. A third possible cause, eruption of fresh pumice from a local volcanic vent, can be eliminated from consideration; there have been no eruptions in Mono Basin in historic times.[15]

Indeed, one must remain skeptical of Leonard's geologic knowledge; it seems possible that he may have mistaken tufa towers projecting above lake waters, or tufa masses and nodules on shore—conditions observable at a number of lakes in the region—for pumice. Perhaps the sighting of pumice should be given the same weight as Leonard's account of the party's capture, two days

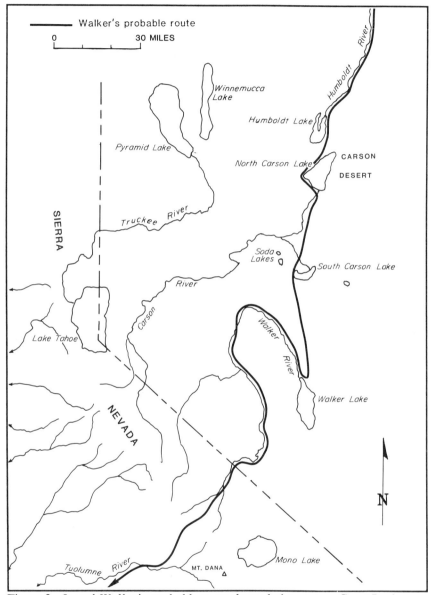

Figure 2. *Joseph Walker's probable route through the western Great Basin.*

later, of a camel—a detail his most recent editor has been at pains to explain as another printer's error.[16]

Once they reached the crest of the Sierra, Walker's party struggled through deep snow in rough country cut by a series of ravines—topography quite unlike that encountered between Mono Basin and Yosemite Valley. That Walker and his companions reached the brink of Yosemite and looked into the valley from the north is the one certain datum that Leonard's narrative of the Sierran crossing provides. Working backward from this reference point, Farquhar also concludes that the party had probably ascended a fork of the Walker River:

> From somewhere west of Tuolumne Meadows the party must have been following the general course of the old Mono Indian trail, in general the route of the present Tioga Road. Before reaching this they had struggled for a number of days through a country of hills, rocks, and snowfields, had found lakes and timberline-type trees. They could not, therefore, have crossed by Bloody Canyon and Mono Pass, nor even Tioga Pass; for if they had, they would not have encountered the rough country described. The answer seems clear. They must have been floundering through the intricate mazes of the northern tributaries of the Tuolumne River. Working backwards, this brings us to the most likely point of crossing the crest, somewhere at the head of East Walker River west of Bridgeport Valley.[17]

Thus, although Walker and his men probably came very close, it cannot be plausibly demonstrated, on the basis of Leonard's *Narrative*, that they reached Mono Lake in 1833.

In subsequent years, Walker crossed and re-crossed the Great Basin and the Sierra Nevada, as he led immigrants into California or accompanied exploratory parties, including Fremont's Third Expedition. It is possible that in these extensive travels he may have looked into or entered Mono Basin, but no record of such a discovery exists. Douglas Watson, in his short biography of Walker, says that after a few years of ranching south of San Francisco Bay, Walker's itchy feet once more got the better of him, so that "in 1854 he organized a party to explore and prospect in the region surrounding Mono Lake."[18] But in 1854 Walker would have been too late to be the first white man to discover Mono Basin and its treasures; he must have been responding to the reports of gold found there by 1st Lt. Tredwell Moore of the Second Infantry in the summer of 1852.

The Discovery of Mono Basin:
Lt. Tredwell Moore's Expedition of 1852

In July, 1852, while leading a detachment of soldiers on a punitive expedition against Chief Teneiya and his band of Yosemite Miwok, Lt. Tredwell Moore of the U.S. Army discovered Mono Basin. Information regarding Lt. Moore's explorations is exceedingly scanty—prior to this research, the only known sources on his activities in the Yosemite and Mono areas were short and somewhat fanciful reports of the expedition published in newspapers after his return, and an account in Bunnell's *Discovery of the Yosemite*, published in 1881, almost thirty years after the events took place. Bunnell's account was based on the testimony of one of Moore's men, Augustus Gray, and has been the principal source for all subsequent discussions of Moore's 1852 activities.

Bunnell was a member of the Mariposa Battalion, which had entered Yosemite Valley on March 27, 1851, and explored it for the first time. It was Bunnell who named the valley "Yosemity," after the Miwok band living there. According to Bunnell the spelling of the name was changed to the modern form "Yosemite" by Lt. Moore in a letter to the *Mariposa Chronicle* in 1854. Unfortunately, neither this letter nor any official report of the expedition have ever been located.

In the course of this research, however, I discovered three previously unknown letters from Lt. Moore to his military superiors at Pacific Division headquarters, written while engaged on his expedition, which had been buried in the holdings of U.S. Army correspondence at the National Archives in Washington D.C. (the full texts are presented in Appendix I, page 95). The letters correct erroneous details and inaccuracies in Bunnell's and subsequent accounts regarding both Moore's route through the area and his actions against the Yosemites.

Lt. Moore was stationed at Fort Miller on the San Joaquin River (near present Fresno; Figure 3, page 20) when word arrived in early June, 1852, that the Yosemite Indians had killed three and wounded two white prospectors on the Merced River. The murders (if such they were) demanded immediate punishment according to the standards of the times; on June 12 Moore wrote to Pacific Division headquarters:

> I will start in pursuit of them Monday next, and endeavor not only to punish the Indians who were engaged in committing the murder, but also to remove the tribe to the reservation set aside for them by the commissioners last year [Appendix I, Letter 1, page 95].

Moore's party consisted of soldiers, volunteer "scouts," some of whom had been friends of the slain miners, and friendly Indian guides who knew the topography.

By the 20th of June, Moore had set up a temporary base camp which he called "Camp Steele" (Letter 2); Bunnell makes no mention of a base of operations.[19] The position of Camp Steele is a critical datum for the reconstruction of Moore's movements in the high country. Moore describes it as "near the Head waters of the Merced," which would seem to indicate some spot in Little Yosemite Valley (Figure 3, page 20). Alternatively, Camp Steele may have been located on the broad divide between the South and Middle Forks of the Merced on the Mono Trail, perhaps near Westfall Meadows.[20] Moore wrote, "Immediately on my arrival scouting parties were sent to scour the country in all directions. Many deserted 'Rancherias' [Indian camps] were found, but no Indians." Moore's letter also reveals that he was working in concert with Major Savage, who was renowned for his role in earlier actions of the Mariposa Indian War. From Camp Steele, Savage led a search-party upstream "from the valley [Little Yosemite?] towards the head waters of the San Joaquin," but had to return empty-handed when his supplies ran out.

On July 1, Lt. Moore dispatched his subordinate Lt. McLean to Yosemite Valley "with instructions to destroy the Rancherias and provisions there." The scouting parties sent out the week before had evidently entered Yosemite Valley and found it empty of Indians, their villages and food-stores abandoned. Also on July 1, Moore left Camp Steele for higher country with the bulk of his men. At first they followed Savage's route of the previous week, but then, discovering a plain trail crossing their path, they turned to follow it, and crossed the "main ridge of the Sierra" on July 4. Moore's scouts quickly located a "rancheria" with 21 Indians still in residence. Moore and his men surrounded and captured them in broad daylight—six men and the rest women and children. The following morning, having found what he considered ample evidence of their complicity in the murders of the prospectors, Moore executed all six men.

The execution of the Yosemites did not take place in Yosemite Valley, as Bunnell's account has it, but somewhere in the high country above. Moore's description of his route is vague, completely lacking in distances and directions. It is clear from the context of Letter 2, however, that by "main ridge of the Sierra" Moore did not mean the actual crest of the range; had he crossed the crest he could only have descended the steep scarp to the desert below, an adventure which still lay before him. But Moore could easily have mistaken the high and rugged Cathedral Range for the actual crest. He was probably led over this sub-

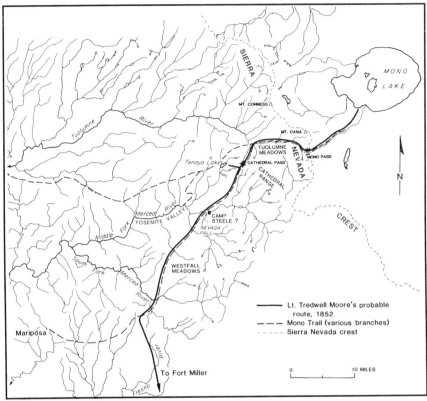

Figure 3. *Lt. Tredwell Moore's probable route into Mono Basin in 1852.*

sidiary massif by his Indian guides via the fork of the Mono Trail passing from Little Yosemite Valley to Tuolumne Meadows; the trail was an Indian thoroughfare. After crossing the "main ridge" (at Cathedral Pass) Moore halted and sent out his scouts, who discovered the rancheria only four miles away, probably near Tenaya Lake, a favorite summer camp of Chief Teneiya and his band. Teneiya and most of his people had already made good their escape; Moore captured a group of stragglers still lingering at the camp (Letter 3).

Bunnell's account, based on Gray's testimony, states that Lt. Moore picked up Chief Teneiya's trail at Tenaya Lake, and followed him into Mono Basin. Letter 3 makes it clear, however, that before Moore could undertake this enterprise, he needed reinforcements. After executing the six men on July 5, he returned to Camp Steele, where on July 8 and 9 he wrote to his superiors informing them of his actions and announcing his intentions:

From information received from the Indian women taken a few days since, I have determined to follow the Yosemites across the Sierras, into the Mono country. The Yo semitis [sic] are on friendly terms with the Monos and have fled to this country thinking that the whites will not follow them across the snow.

Moore requested additional men and ten six-shooters so that his expedition could be carried out in safety (one of his men, under the command of Lt. McLean, had been killed by an arrow in Yosemite Valley). Moore dispatched one of his subordinates, Lt. Crosby, to carry his requisitions to Pacific Division headquarters at Benicia (Appendix II, Item 2, page 99).

Unfortunately, at this point Lt. Moore's letters end. An extensive search of National Archives records failed to turn up any additional information; no official report describing later stages of the expedition seems to exist.[21] Except for the less reliable newspaper reports, Bunnell's account must remain the only source of information on Moore's further movements.

According to Bunnell, after picking up Chief Teneiya's trail at Tenaya Lake,

Lieutenant Moore crossed the Sierras over the Mono trail that leads by the Soda Springs through the Mono Pass. He made some fair discoveries of gold and gold-bearing quartz, obsidian, and other minerals, while exploring the region north and south of Bloody Canyon and of Mono Lake. Finding no trace whatever of the cunning chief, he returned to the Soda Springs, and from there took his homeward journey to Fort Miller by way of the old trail that passed to the south of the Yosemite.[22]

Although Bunnell gives few details of Moore's movements inside Mono Basin, his mention of the "old trail" from Soda Springs (at Tuolumne Meadows) passing south of Yosemite lends support to the reconstruction of Moore's earlier route over the Cathedral Range. Both in entering and in leaving Mono Basin and the high Yosemite country, Moore followed the south branch of the Mono Trail.

Interestingly, though Bunnell does not mention who discovered the Mono Lake country, he states unequivocally that Lt. Moore did not. Perhaps Bunnell believed that Jedediah Smith or Joseph Walker had already visited the region. Or perhaps a passage in Moore's letter of July 9 (Appendix I, Letter 3, page 97) contains a clue: "The Indians inform me that mules can be taken across the mountains without much difficulty." Had prospectors already crossed Mono Pass with mules? Or had the Yosemite Miwok themselves taken up the use of them? The possibility that some small party of whites had preceded Moore cannot be ruled out. In any case, Lt. Tredwell Moore remains the leader of the first white party definitely known to have entered Mono Basin.

Moore's explorations immediately stimulated further penetrations of the basin by his countrymen. His status as an officer of the Regular Army lent credence to his reports on the Mono country.[23] When he displayed samples of the gold he had found in the basin to prospectors in Mariposa, he met with an enthusiastic audience. According to Bunnell,

> Leroy Vining, and a few chosen companions, with one of Moore's scouts as guide, went over the Sierras to the place where the gold had been found, and established themselves on what has since been known as Vining's Gulch or Creek.[23]

Thus, Moore's report of his travels led directly to the first white settlement in the basin.

Moore's explorations were widely publicized in newspapers in San Francisco and Stockton in August 1852. The least fanciful account, based on information from Lt. Crosby, contains the first published description of Mono Lake:

> After descending into the plains and marching a short distance in search of Indians, they discovered, about fifteen miles from the base of the hills, a large lake some twenty-five or thirty miles long, by the same measurement in width, which they named Lake Mono, after the tribe of Indians that inhabit that section. This lake does not appear to have any outlet, and is of a very brackish taste. There are several streams of pure water—two of considerable magnitude—emptying into it, on the borders of which is the only wood to be found. Sea gulls, geese, and ducks abound on its waters, and its banks are covered with *tache le mere* and sand [full text in Appendix II, Item 1, page 98].

In 1853, as a result of the information brought back by Moore, Mono Lake was shown for the first time on a published map, Trask's *Map of the State of California*. The map depicts an elongated water body with a northwest-southeast trend, in the correct location, and with the name "Mono Lake." No islands are shown.

The following year, 1854, a more recognizable Mono Lake appeared on Eddy's *Official Map of the State of California*. At the bottom of the map a long list of "Authorities" for the information presented is given, including the following:

> The Mono Country is from a sketch by the discoverers, Lieuts. J. [sic] Moore and N. H. McLean, U.S. Army.

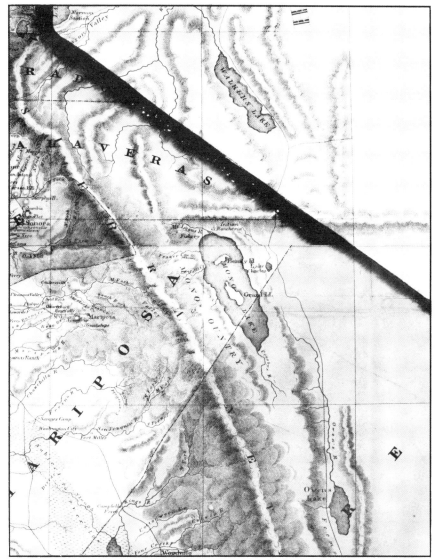

Figure 4. *A portion of Eddy's "Official Map of the State of California" (1854). Courtesy, the Bancroft Library.*

The representation of the lake is not entirely accurate; its long axis is shown running about 90 degrees from its actual orientation, and the general shape of the lake is exaggeratedly elongated. Nevertheless, the depiction is an improvement over that of the Trask map of the year before; Eddy's map clearly shows the two large islands in the middle of the lake and a number of the tributary streams around it, all given names supplied by Lt. Moore (Figure 4, page 23).[25] By placing Mono Basin on the map and in the minds of Californians, Lt. Tredwell Moore raised the curtain on a new stage, whose attractions would not long go unappreciated.

The First Surveys: A. W. von Schmidt

Less than three years after Lt. Moore's return to Mariposa, on May 30, 1855, Alexis W. von Schmidt signed a contract with the Surveyor General of the United States for the State of California, John C. Hays, to undertake the extension of the survey of the Mt. Diablo baseline to the vicinity of the eastern boundary of California. The exact location of the California-Nevada boundary line itself had not yet been established (the first attempts to locate it precisely were not made until 1863), nor had any part of California east of the Sierra Nevada been surveyed. It was therefore necessary to begin the task of surveying east of the mountains by extending the baseline beyond them. The U.S. Land Office thought the lands had agricultural potential; part of von Schmidt's contract called for him to estimate soil fertility and water availability in the country he should survey. The baseline extension took von Schmidt and his assistants into the middle of Mono Basin, where they established the baseline some three miles south of Mono Lake. They surveyed eastward into Range 31 E., several miles beyond the lake but short of the state line, finishing the extension on July 7, 1855.

The survey had been difficult, especially in the Sierra Nevada. Rough terrain forced von Schmidt to offset from the baseline frequently, and at times to remain away for a number of miles, running a line parallel to it until the topography should allow a return to the baseline itself.[26] His party had difficulty in keeping surveyors and pack animals in communication, and more than once members of the party bivouacked without food for two or three days after the topography had forced a separation between surveyors and pack train. After an especially difficult crossing of Kuna Crest, made just south of Helen Lake, von Schmidt descended into Mono Basin via Bloody Canyon, from the head of which he had his first sight of Mono Lake:

The eastern side of this mountain is almost perpendicular. This being the Eastern Ridge of the Sierra Nevada Mountains, which bears off S by E. From this point the

Alexis W. von Schmidt. Courtesy, the California State Library.

view of the country lying East and S. East is magnificent. Mono Lake with its two Islands lying to the NE looks beautiful—and in short—take the scenery altogether is the most beautiful that I ever saw.[27]

After finishing the baseline extension, von Schmidt spent another week establishing the first, second and third standard lines south of the baseline, as specified in his contract. He drew a sketch map of Mono Lake and the lands he

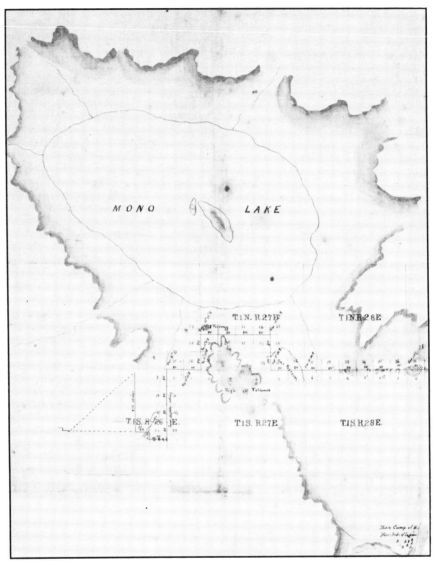

Figure 5. *A portion of von Schmidt's sketch-map of the Mt. Diablo baseline extension (1855). Courtesy, the Bancroft Library.*

had surveyed to the south, which is now in the possession of the Bancroft Library (a portion of it is reproduced here as Figure 5, page 26). Von Schmidt located "The Main Camp of the Mono Tribe of Indians" at the head of Owens River, showed the Mono Craters extending south from Mono Lake, and clearly depicted the lake's two large islands lying far from shore. He also sketched in Rush, Lee Vining, Mill, Wilson and Cottonwood creeks in reasonably true locations, but without naming them. On his survey plats, Rush and Lee Vining creeks were given the names "Lake" and "Rescue" creeks respectively. The name Rescue Creek may have derived from one of the misadventures suffered by his men while trying to cross the crest of the range. On his return to Sacramento at the beginning of August an account of his expedition appeared in the *Sacramento Daily Union* (Appendix 2, Item 3, page 99), highlighting the difficulties he had encountered.

On August 13, 1856, a year later, von Schmidt signed another contract with the Surveyor General to carry out a more detailed survey of Mono Basin and the land south into Owens Valley. The work contracted for required three more trips across the Sierra Nevada, in August 1856, January 1857 and July 1857. Von Schmidt did not take the Bloody Canyon route again, preferring the easier entry afforded by Sonora or Emigrant passes.

Wherever undertaken, von Schmidt's surveys were carried on in a highly professional manner and were remarkably accurate, especially in view of the adverse physical and social conditions under which he and his assistants were often forced to operate. His observations of the Paiute of Owens Valley have been of great value in determining their numbers, distribution and modes of life at this early contact period;[28] it is unfortunate that his notes contain no information on the Kuzedika of Mono Lake. In addition, his surveys of Owens Valley have enabled modern researchers to locate and establish minimum ages for the extensive irrigation canals constructed by the Paiute for their own indigenous system of agriculture, a phenomenon of considerable interest to students of Indian agriculture in the western United States.[29] Finally, his meander survey of the shore of Mono Lake has allowed reconstruction of the surface elevation of the lake in 1857 to within an accuracy of one foot;[30] this information has been critical in determining how dramatically Mono Lake rises and falls in response to natural climatic fluctuations.[31]

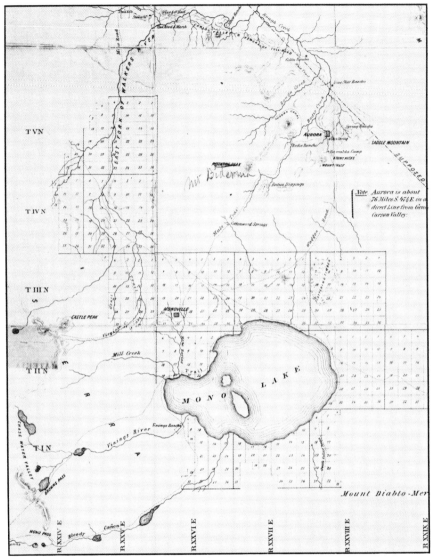

Figure 6. *A portion of Clayton's "Map of Esmeralda and Mono" (1861). Courtesy, the Bancroft Library.*

Chapter 3

EARLY SETTLEMENT, 1852-1877

Dogtown, Monoville and Aurora

When Lt. Moore returned from Mono Basin in August, 1852, after failing to capture Chief Teneiya and his band, he stopped in Mariposa to exhibit samples of the gold his party had discovered north of Bloody Canyon. The exhibits were impressive enough to spur Leroy Vining and a few companions to settle in the basin and begin prospecting in the fall of 1852.[1] Where they worked is not known; according to Bunnell they established themselves in Lee Vining Canyon. It is probable, however, that they prospected a greater area, perhaps working the slopes north of Mono Lake, or ground north of the drainage divide in the East Walker River basin, where significant placer deposits were found a few years later. In 1855, State Geologist John B. Trask, in a report to the legislature of California concerning mining in the state, noted promising developments on the east side of the Sierra Nevada:

In my report of last year, it was stated that the placer ranges were at that time known to extend nearly to the summit ridge of the mountains; but this year it has been ascertained that they pass beyond the ridge and are found on the eastern declivity...Within the past season, many of these deposits have been examined, and thus far are found to be equally productive with those...to the west, and, with a favorable season ensuing, they will be largely occupied.

Carl P. Russell, an authority on the history of the Yosemite region, considered it probable that Trask based his statement upon reports from Lee Vining's party in Mono Basin.[2]

Evidently Vining found little gold, however, because few people were attracted to the area until the discovery of the Dogtown placers in 1857. Credit for this discovery goes to Mormon prospectors from the north. After establishing the settlement of Mormon Station (later Genoa), Nevada in 1850 (Figure 7, page 45), they worked slowly southward along the east side of the Sierra Nevada year by year, prospecting as they went.[3] The Dogtown placers lay just north of the Mono Basin in the East Walker River watershed, extending upstream along Virginia Creek from its confluence with Clearwater Creek to its junction with Dog Creek (formerly Dogtown Creek), and up Dog Creek for about three miles.[4]

The Dogtown deposits created considerable excitement among miners in the foothills west of the Sierra, where profits from the placers had been steadily diminishing. Men rushed to Dogtown from Sonora, Columbia, Chinese Camp and Jamestown over the Emigrant Pass route,[5] from the Mariposa area over the Mono Trail,[6] and even from Visalia in the southern San Joaquin Valley via Walker Pass and Owens Valley.[7] As many as one hundred men worked the Dogtown placers in the years 1857 to 1859 during periods of favorable weather and stream flow.[8] Typically, the miners would arrive from the west side in late spring and work until fall, recrossing the mountains before the onset of the first major storms. Since Dog and Virginia creeks maintain flows throughout the dry season, there was ample water for working the placers. All operations were carried out with simple rockers; none of the more advanced techniques developed west of the Sierra were employed.[9] At least one store was established at Dogtown which, like the miner's cabins, had a stone foundation and walls of cottonwood logs chinked with mud.[10] The foundations of some of these structures can still be seen near the confluence of Virginia and Clearwater creeks next to U.S. 395.[11]

The Dogtown strike familiarized men west of the Sierra with the Mono region for the first time, and made several routes of entry to the area well known. In the spring of 1859 word spread among west-side miners that even richer placers had been discovered in Mono Gulch, a steep, bouldery ravine between Conway Summit and Mono Lake. Another rush occurred, dwarfing the earlier one to Dogtown. Led by veterans of the Dogtown excitement, miners came to the new "Mono Diggings" from the Tuolumne and Mariposa county mines over Emigrant and Mono passes, from the southern San Joaquin Valley via Walker Pass, and from the Carson Valley and Lake Tahoe regions south along the forks of the Walker River (Figure 7, page 45). The town that quickly sprang up was called Monoville.

The Monoville rush clearly preceded the strike of the Comstock Lode in June, 1859, but the exact date of discovery of the Mono Diggings cannot be determined. Lee Vining and his party may have worked the area prior to the spring of 1859 when the rush was underway. Local legend gives the credit to Cord Norst, who claimed to have made the discovery on July 4th or 5th, 1859.[12] His claim must be spurious, however, because by spring of 1859 the population of Mono Diggings had already topped 70.[13] For the excitement to have brought miners east over the Sierra that spring, the discovery must have been made no later than the previous year in the summer or fall of 1858.

The miners encountered a number of hindrances to working the placers at Monoville, foremost among them a lack of water. The diggings were located along the beds and banks of ephemeral streams descending the flank of the Bodie Hills toward the northwest corner of Mono Lake. Henry Degroot, a mining expert, visited Monoville in late 1859 and made this report in 1860:[14]

> While the diggings are tolerably extensive, and certainly rich, there is but little water. By the time the snow has so far disappeared as to admit of travel over the mountains, the streams have subsided to an extent that leaves water but for a small number of miners. Thus it was that while extensive dry and gulch diggings were known to exist on the benches and along the ravines, only about two hundred men found opportunity to work in this district last season [summer, 1859]. A ditch, however, has been completed, bringing in water to Mono Camp, and others will probably be constructed the coming summer, whereby this prime obstacle to successful operations will be, to some extent, overcome.[15]

The lack of water caused many men to leave Monoville and head elsewhere. In the words of R. K. Colcord, and early arrival and reliable informant:

> I found little encouragement to prospect for gold in the district as there was scarcely water enough for rockers after September, though a few men made money sluicing earlier in the season. Nearly the entire outfit left the country before the storms commenced and returned to the western slope.[16]

For those able to acquire sufficient water, the Mono Diggings were profitable; earnings there were three or four times higher than the average take of the common miner west of the crest. At Monoville, according to DeGroot,

"Town of Mono" (Monoville) in 1863 as sketched by J. Ross Browne.

the average return per miner per day was about $12, and sometimes rose as high as $20; on the west side the average was down to $3 per day by 1859.[17] Thus there was a strong incentive to bring water to the rich placers; ditch digging, as noted by DeGroot, was well underway in 1859. Construction of a ditch from Virginia Creek in the East Walker River watershed began in 1858; when completed in 1859, the ditch crossed the drainage divide into Mono Basin just west of Conway Summit.[18] A second ditch, following the same general route as the first, was built between June and October of 1860 at a reported cost of $75,000 (Figure 9, page 55).[19]

But the miners had other problems besides a lack of water, all of which DeGroot pointed out in his pamphlet:

There are other hindrances that should discourage emigration to these remote and uncertain mines. These may be summed up briefly, as follows: the great distance, the shortness of the season, and the expense of living. From San Francisco to these mines, going by Sonora, the most direct route, is 330 miles. But the mountains by this route cannot be crossed till June, wherefore the journey, if undertaken sooner, must be made by the circuitous way of Walker or Kern river, either of which will increase the distance to more than 400 miles. Eight months in the year is as long as we can calculate for the working season in the Mono country, while the cost of living will be, at least, three times as great as in the mines of California. Keeping these drawbacks in view, it is for each man canvassing the question, to determine for himself what may be the chances of success, and what, in his particular case, the inducements for visiting these mines. It should be added, that so far as there is water for working, the mining grounds are already taken up, and even much more has been claimed in anticipation of water being hereafter brought in.[20]

There is no way of knowing how many men were discouraged from coming to Monoville by DeGroot's singularly objective report. The town continued to swell through 1860; population estimates for that year range from 900 to 3,000.[21] Since mining alone could not support such numbers, many men gave up mining for ditch digging at a daily wage, cutting timber, packing in supplies, running (or patronizing) saloons and gambling.

Another alternative was to prospect elsewhere in the vicinity. This was the choice of W. S. "Bill" Body and his companions, who had come to the diggings from Sonora in 1859 only to find a horde of men taking up every inch of workable ground. Body and his partner, E. S. "Black" Taylor, prospected east of Monoville in the high rolling country later to be known as the Bodie Hills. Body and Taylor found placers in the bottom of a gulch about 15 miles northeast of Monoville, staked a claim, and began to provision themselves for the winter there, making repeated trips to Monoville for supplies. According to Joseph Wasson, whose pamphlet *Bodie and Esmeralda* (1878) is the earliest reliable account of the genesis and rise of the town of Bodie, the two men were caught in a severe blizzard in March 1860 while returning to their cabin from Monoville. They were separated by the storm; Taylor managed to reach the cabin and survived, but Body froze to death in Cottonwood Canyon. His remains were found in May after the snow had melted by miners attracted to his placer discovery. Shortly afterward they named their camp and district Bodie in his honor (with a slight change of spelling).

Body's demise exemplifies the harshness of early living conditions in the area. J. Ross Browne, who passed through the Bodie camp in 1864, gave a vivid description of the typical miner's home in the region:

Usually it is constructed of the materials nearest at hand. Stone and mud answer for the walls where wood is scarce; but if wood be abundant, a kind of stockade is formed of logs placed close together and upright in the ground. The roof is made of clapboards, or rough shingles, brushwood covered with sod, canvas, or anything else that may be available. I have seen roofs constructed of flour-sacks, cast-off shirts, coats, and pantaloons, all sewed together like a home-made quilt...The chimney is the most imposing part of the house. Where the location permits, the cabin is backed up against a bluff, so as to afford a chance for a substantial flue by merely cutting a hole through the bank; but where such natural facilities do not exist, the variety of material used in the construction of chimneys is wonderful. Stone, wood, scraps of sheet-iron, adobe-bricks, mud, whisky-barrels, nail-kegs, and even canvas are the component parts.[22]

As long as the placers proved profitable, or at least promised to be so, miners would put up with any discomforts. But as soon as it became clear that they were unlikely to strike it rich, it was off to the next "excitement." And off they went in great numbers in the late fall of 1860 to a new discovery at Esmeralda, soon to be re-named Aurora, some 25 miles northeast of Monoville, hoping again for easy wealth (Figure 7, page 45).

The Aurora strike overshadowed the new developments at Bodie, and spelled the end of the Monoville boom. In the summer of 1861 many of Monoville's buildings were taken down and rebuilt in Aurora. Some placering must have continued in the Mono Diggings, however, because in the first general election in the newly created Mono County, held in September, 337 votes were cast at Monoville.[23] The Monoville placers were not totally depleted. All work had been done with rockers and sluices; the tailings from such crude devices still contained considerable quantities of gold. Furthermore, the tailings had spread over other unworked placers downstream which could still yield profits. Placers also still existed beneath the enormous granite boulders that littered the gulches and could not be removed by miners so simply equipped. These protected placers still promised rich yields if they could be worked hydraulically, and in later years hydraulic operations in the Mono Diggings did develop (see page 70). The miners who left knew that wealth still lay in the ground at Monoville, and some returned in later years and carried on there quietly. But by 1862 the town of Monoville was no more. The total yield of the Monoville placers was estimated at several million dollars,[24] but since no records of the actual production are preserved, there is no way to substantiate this estimate.[25]

The Aurora bonanza dwarfed the excitements at Monoville and Dogtown. Rich silver veins near the surface promised great and easily-won wealth. In 1861 the town was chosen to be the seat of newly-formed Mono County, and the first stamp-mill was built there.[26] By 1863 sixteen mills were in operation separating the silver from the gangue, or waste-rock. In the spring of 1863 the population was over 3,000, and by midsummer it had risen to about 5,000.[27] The influx of people stimulated a variety of developments in the surrounding region: roads to make access and supply easier, an active timber-cutting industry, and farms to provide produce and meat for the miners. Aurora depended upon a large surrounding area for its supplies, including the Mono Basin.

William H. Brewer, a member of the California Geological Survey headed by J. D. Whitney, visited the Mono Basin and Aurora in July of 1863 during the height of the boom. He reported that trains of pack animals carrying supplies to Aurora passed over Mono Pass and down Bloody Canyon every week.[28] The merchants in Mariposa, Coulterville and Big Oak Flat had no choice but to ship freight to Aurora over Mono Pass because other routes would involve much greater distances; but they found the Bloody Canyon trail a cruel one, as Brewer noted:

> After crossing the pass, the way leads down Bloody Canyon—a terrible trail. You would pronounce it utterly inaccessible to horses, yet pack trains come down, but the bones of several horses or mules and the stench of another told that all had not passed safely. The trail comes down three thousand feet in less than four miles, over rocks and loose stones, in narrow canyons and along by precipices. It was a bold man who first took a horse up there. The horses were so cut by sharp rocks that they named it Bloody Canyon, and it has held the name—and it is appropriate—part of the way the rocks in the trail are literally sprinkled with blood from the animals.[29]

John Muir agreed with Brewer about the roughness of the Bloody Canyon trail. He first descended the canyon in 1869, and later described its difficulties at length:

> I have never known an animal, either mule or horse, to make its way through the canyon, either in going up or down, without losing more or less blood from wounds on the legs. Occasionally one is killed outright—falling headlong and rolling over precipices like a boulder. But such accidents are rarer than from the terrible appearance of the trail one would be led to expect; the more experienced when driven loose find their way over the dangerous places with a caution and sagacity that is truly wonderful. During the gold excitement it was at times a matter of considerable pecuniary importance to force a way through the canyon with pack-trains early in the spring while it was yet heavily blocked with snow; and then the mules with their loads had sometimes to be let down over the steepest drifts and avalanche beds by means of ropes.[30]

So much traffic crossed Emigrant and Sonora passes bound for Aurora that the Mono County Board of Supervisors decided to undertake construction of a wagon road over the crest. The Sonora and Mono Road over Sonora Pass was begun in 1863, and took five years to complete at a cost of over $400,000.[31] Other wagon roads linked Aurora with Carson Valley to the north and with Big Meadows (later Bridgeport) to the west, where large stock-raising and timber-cutting operations had developed.[32]

J. Ross Browne. Courtesy, the Bancroft Library.

The hungry population of Aurora stimulated the establishment of farms in well-watered spots within a radius of at least thirty miles. According to J. Ross Browne, by 1864 every suitable place was in agricultural production:

Several fine valleys, now used as hay and cattle ranches, lie between Bodie and Aurora. They are small, but rich in soil and well watered by the springs that course down from the neighboring ravines, and produce some fine grass. The ranchmen were at work hauling the hay to the Aurora market, where it brings from $40 to $60 a ton. Hay ranches are as good as silver mines almost anywhere on the eastern slope—better, in some respects, for they are certain to yield something for the labor expended upon them...In respect to the article of provisions, the proximity of Big

Meadows, Mono Lake, and Walker's Valley, where vegetable products of all kinds are now abundantly raised, is a great advantage to this district. Until within a year or two miners suffered much from the want of vegetables; scurvy was a common disease; but during the past summer the supply has been quite equal to the demand. Farms are being located and cultivated in all the adjacent valleys, where the altitude is not too great for agricultural purposes...There are some twenty settlers living on the shores of Lake Mono, most of whom are engaged in stock-raising and hay-cutting...Most of the lands available for cultivation have been taken up. These are timbered, or adjacent to timber, and are well watered by springs. A sawmill has recently been erected, and now that there is a chance of getting lumber it is probable a number of new houses will be built during the next summer.[33]

In addition to hay, meat and vegetables, settlers in the Mono Basin supplied Aurora with gulls' eggs from the islands in the lake where the birds bred each spring. The eggs commanded a price of from $1 to $1.50 a dozen. The business was necessarily a seasonal one.[34]

In 1861, and possibly for some time before that date, Lee Vining operated a sawmill in the canyon named after him, where he cut timber for the Aurora market. "Vinings Rancho" is shown on Clayton's 1861 "Map of Esmeralda and Mono," the first published map to show accurately the configuration of Mono Lake, the location of its tributary streams and the sites of Monoville, Bodie and Esmeralda (Aurora); a portion is reproduced as Figure 6, page 28.[35] Vining died in Aurora when, after delivering a shipment of lumber, his pistol accidentally went off in his pocket.[36]

This unfortunate incident, however, saved Vining from witnessing an inevitable turn for the worse in his lumber business, because by 1865 Aurora had played itself out. Aurora's decline had actually started in 1863, the moment of its greatest apparent prosperity, when it became evident that in most of the major mines the ores diminished rapidly with depth. In 1865 gold and silver bullion shipments fell off drastically, and most of the mines closed.[37] Aurora and its supporting hinterland fell quiet for more than a decade.

The Quiet Period, 1865-1877

When the mines at Aurora closed in 1865, the base of the local economy disappeared; when the miners left, the merchants followed. Aurora's demand for local products, such as meat, milk, cheese, butter, vegetables, eggs, lumber and cord-wood, fell off drastically. Like the newly unemployed miners, those whose livelihood depended upon the Aurora market had to move on or adjust to the new conditions. Most moved on—from a peak of 5,000 people at Aurora in 1863, the population of the region dwindled, until in 1877 only 1,000 people lived in all of Mono County,[38] and just a fraction of these within Mono Basin. From 1865 to 1877, the economy of the basin was largely a self-contained one, a condition imposed by isolation and the lack of a mercantile center, such as booming Aurora had been.

During this quiet period some mining continued—a few men at Bodie, a few at Aurora, and others scattered here and there working or re-working placer deposits. According to DeGroot, during every summer after 1860 placering was carried on along the foot of the Sierra between Bridgeport and the head-waters of the Owens River. The placer deposits existed both along the base of the mountains and in the canyons at elevations as high as 4,000 feet above the floors of the east-side basins. In the narrow ravines the placers were worked by sluices and rockers exclusively, but the lower deposits were worked hydraulically as well.[39] Joseph LeConte, visiting Mono Basin in 1870, observed hydraulic mining in the old Dogtown diggings.[40] Some of the placers which had been abandoned by whites were taken up by Chinese miners; J. Ross Browne saw them placering in Cottonwood Canyon south of Bodie in 1864, and LeConte described their little village of mud and stone huts, each with its irrigated vegetable garden, at Dogtown in 1870.[41] The gold from these workings was shipped to Carson City and San Francisco, and provided a cash flow for the Mono area—a continuous trickle of money which facilitated local trade.

But the principal activities in the basin during these quiet years were farming and stock-raising. Attracted by reports of good land around Mono Lake, a slow stream of settlers began to flow into the Mono Basin in the early 1860s. Most of them located their homesteads along the lower courses of the streams draining the Sierra Nevada—Wilson, Mill, Lee Vining, Rush, Walker and Parker creeks—where they could take advantage of natural meadowlands. Others settled flat open spots within the Sierran canyons, including Lundy Canyon, Lee Vining Canyon and below Walker Lake in Bloody Canyon, and near scattered springs around Mono Lake, such as Warford Springs to the north, Warm Springs to the east and Sammon (now Simons) Spring to the southeast.

In better-drained parts of the meadows, or on irrigated land that had been cleared of sagebrush, the settlers grew hay, alfalfa, wheat, barley and oats; they also raised a variety of vegetables in gardens around the farmhouses. Cattle, sheep and horses grazed in the meadows and on the sagebrush slopes, which contained many succulent grasses and forbs. The land was largely unfenced, and every inch of the north, west and south slopes of the basin, wherever stock animals could keep their feet, was undoubtedly heavily grazed.

Mono Lake provided a bounteous seasonal supply of meat to the pioneers. In the late summer and fall vast numbers of ducks and other migratory waterfowl rested from their long flights at Mono Lake. The settlers, armed with shotguns, killed them in quantity for their meat and feathers.

These early pioneers had an abundant and varied diet. The "harsh desert" and the "dead sea" provided lives of plenty—plenty of meat, vegetables, milk, butter, cheese and wool. J. Ross Browne, who visited a farm on Mono Lake's north shore in 1864, was impressed by the quality of life:

> It was a pleasant, home-looking place, with haystacks, wagons, and lowing cattle about the farmyard...The house was a snug frame shanty, containing three or four rooms, roughly but comfortably furnished...Beds were plenty—deep, full feather beds, in which the sleeper was luxuriously buried for the night. I found that feathers were a staple product here...[The] supper would have done honor to the best hotel in New York...such delicately flavored mutton, such rich yellow cream, such pure fresh milk and sparkling butter...The biscuits, too, were delicious; and there were preserves of wild mountain berries, and jams and tarts an pies...as for vegetables, there was any variety; and the potatoes were as rich and mealy as the best Irish murphies.[42]

Most of the homesteads around Mono Lake were usually able to produce more meat, hay and vegetables than they needed, and so had a surplus for trade. The farmers traded and bartered among themselves, and supplied the small population of miners in the surrounding area with food as well. Travelling traders from west of the Sierra came into the basin in the summertime after the Sonora and Mono Road was completed in 1868. Merchants with wagon-loads of fruit—peaches, apples and grapes—made the long trip over Sonora Pass, sure of brisk business when they reached the fruit-starved Mono Lake settlers.[43] Visitors to the basin—such as John Muir, who made the first of many visits in 1869, and Joseph LeConte, who first came in 1870—could depend upon getting mutton, corned beef, milk, cheese and other food from the settlers.[44]

Trade and barter eventually developed between the settlers and the native inhabitants, the Kuzedika Paiute. When the whites first entered the basin in large numbers in the late 1850s, the Kuzedika avoided them completely, temporarily abandoning the north and west shores of Mono Lake. Gradually, however, they returned, and tried to live there as they had before.[45] But the continuing presence of the whites—first the hordes of miners at Monoville, then the large numbers passing to and from Aurora and the settlers occupying the fertile spots in the basin—forced the Kuzedika into a slow process of adaptation to

John Muir visiting a Kuzedika camp on the northwest shore of Mono Lake. Photograph by C. Hart Merriam, circa 1900. Courtesy, the Bancroft Library.

new conditions, a process which some of them, especially the elders, resisted. Joseph LeConte noted a "generation gap" in the attitude of the Kuzedika toward the whites:

> Several Indians visited us while at dinner. This is a favorite time for such visits. They know they will get something to eat. Two younger Indians were full of life and good-nature, but one old wrinkled fellow was very reticent, and stood much upon his dignity. He had a beautiful bow and several arrows. We put up some bread and the younger ones shot for it; but the old Indian would take no notice of it, and even seemed to treat the idea with contempt. He evidently belongs to the "Old Regime." He remembers the time when the noble red man had undisputed possession of this part of the country.[46]

The activities of the whites greatly reduced the Kuzedika's food-supply, and restricted their freedom of movement as well. The settlers collected gull eggs by the thousands from the islands, cut pinyon pines for fuel, grazed their stock on the wild grasses, killed or scared the deer and antelope, and preyed heavily on the waterfowl. As the whites moved in and claimed the best land, the Kuzedika were forced away from their favorite spring and summer camps. Finding it increasingly difficult to procure their traditional foods, they became more and more dependent upon the white settlers for food-stuffs, horses, guns, tobacco, whisky and other commodities.[47] The Kuzedika had always been traders; it was a simple step, although not a painless one, for them to broaden their trade network to include the whites. For the products they desired, they traded venison, pinenuts, baskets, fish and ducks.[48]

Even as these changes were forced upon them, the Kuzedika held onto many aspects of their traditional way of life. They continued to collect *kutsavi* and caterpillars, drive rabbits and visit their allies the Miwok. In 1869, 17 years after Lee Vining settled in the basin, John Muir was still able to observe Kuzedika women harvesting wildrye in the age-old way:

> Four or five miles from the lake [at the foot of Bloody Canyon] I came to a patch of elymus, or wild rye, growing in magnificent waving clumps six or eight feet high, bearing heads six or eight inches long. The crop was ripe, and Indian women were gathering the grain in baskets by bending down large handfuls, beating out the seed, and fanning it in the wind. The grains are about five-eights of an inch long, dark-colored and sweet. I fancy the bread made from it must be as good as wheat bread. A fine squirrelish employment this wild grain gathering seems, and the women were evidently enjoying it, laughing and chattering.[49]

As time went on, the Kuzedika began to trade their labor for goods. It is impossible to say when they first began to work on the white farms, but by the mid-1880s, Kuzedika men were indispensable hands during sagebrush-clearing, fence-building and the summer-long haying, and the women were employed at washing, threshing and winnowing the harvested grain with their distinctive winnowing baskets.[50] This employer-employee relationship between the white farmers and the Kuzedika must have developed during the 1870s to have been so well-established ten years later.

The Kuzedika's labor on the farms fit into gaps in their own round of activities. When the pinenuts ripened in early fall, the Kuzedika left the white farms to see to their own harvest:

> When the crop is ripe, the Indians make ready the long beating poles; bags, baskets, mats, and sacks are collected; the women out at service among the settlers, washing and drudging, assemble at the family huts; the men leave their ranch work; old and young, all are mounted on ponies and start in great glee to the nut-lands, forming curiously picturesque cavalcades; flaming scarfs and calico skirts stream loosely over the knotty ponies, two squaws usually astride of each, with baby midgets

bandaged in baskets slung on their backs or balanced on the saddle-bow; while nut-baskets and water-jars project from each side, and the long beating-poles make angles in every direction. Arriving at some well-known central point where grass and water are found, the squaws with baskets, the men with poles ascend the ridges to the laden trees, followed by the children. Then the beating begins right merrily, the burs fly in every direction, rolling down the slopes, lodging here and there against rocks and sagebushes, chased and gathered by the women and children with fine natural gladness. Smoke-columns speedily mark the joyful scene of their labors as the roasting-fires are kindled, and, at night, assembled in gay circles a garrulous as jays, they begin the first nut feast of the season.[51]

By 1877, when the rush to Bodie brought the "quiet period" to an end, the Mono Basin settlers had laid the foundations of an agricultural economy capable of producing surplus meat, vegetables and grains. Moreover, in the Kuzedika, they had a cheap, local labor force which would help them make the most of the lucrative market which Bodie so suddenly presented.

Chapter 4

Boom and Bust: 1877-1900

Bodie

For almost two decades, before Bodie suddenly boomed in 1877, its history had been one of hardship, frustration and disappointment. The camp struggled along, year after year, near the site of the original location of gold placers by Body and Taylor in 1859. A few miners' shacks lay in a flat, open valley at 8375 feet, about a mile north of the head of Cottonwood Canyon and about ten miles north of Mono Lake (Figure 1, page xviii). This valley lies just inside the East Walker River basin, and drains to the north by ephemeral Bodie Creek. A total lack of trees and the open, rolling topography of the surrounding hills left Bodie exposed to strong, often cold winds. Midwinter temperatures commonly fall as low as -30 degrees fahrenheit and occasionally even lower, and snow drifts to great depths. The miner's life at Bodie was a difficult one.

The gold deposits discovered by Body and Taylor in 1859 were not true placer deposits, as they had not been significantly transported by stream-flow; they were actually the surface weathering products of local veins. When work first got underway in the spring of 1860, the miners used rockers and pans as they had at Monoville, taking advantage of the snowmelt. As the summer progressed the shortage of water became an acute problem. Soon, however, the miners located outcrops of the veins themselves; because of the lack of water they gave up on the placers and turned to vein mining. The first tunnels at Bodie were begun during the summer of 1860.[1]

The Bodie Mining District was organized in July, 1860, and extended five miles in all directions from the location of Body's initial discovery in Taylor Gulch.[2] The primary ground of the district lay along the backbone of a north-south trending ridge east of the camp called Bodie Bluff. The organization of the Bodie District preceded by a few months the much greater developments at Esmeralda (Aurora), about ten miles to the northeast. The Bodie claims held promise, but they did not compare to the rich silver lodes of Esmeralda. In 1863, when the population of Aurora had swollen to over 5,000 people, a few lonely die-hards were vainly struggling to make Bodie's mines pay.

The timing of the Aurora strike was unfortunate for Bodie, for it attracted capital elsewhere at a critical moment and undermined the costly work of exploration. Money had fairly inundated Aurora. Numerous exploratory tunnels were run, and because the rich silver-bearing veins were all located very close to the surface, success came quickly. By 1863, when 16 costly stamp-mills were in continuous operation, millions of dollars had been invested.

The picture at Bodie contrasted sharply. Not until 1863, after three years of lonely and inadequately financed work, did the miners succeed in attracting outside capital. In that year the Bodie Bluff Consolidated Mining Company was incorporated, with Governor Leland Stanford as president. The stock issue amounted to slightly over $1 million on paper, but the actual working capital was much less. The hoped-for quick profits failed to materialize, and the company failed the next year.[3]

Then, in 1864, a group of New York capitalists decided to give Bodie a try. They bought out a handful of small companies that had been formed by local miners to work claims on Bodie Bluff, and formed the Empire Gold and Silver Mining Company of New York, with $10 million in capital on paper and between $300,000 and $500,000 actually subscribed. In the company's prospectus, two respected mining engineers—Benjamin Silliman Jr. of Yale and William P. Blake of California—reported their first-hand observations. The two men agreed that the Bodie mines held great promise; their conclusions encouraged the New Yorkers to forge ahead.

Silliman's report suggests that the company hoped to operate on a grand scale. Noting that the "placers" along the lower slopes of Bodie Bluff were rich, Silliman detailed plans for their exploitation:

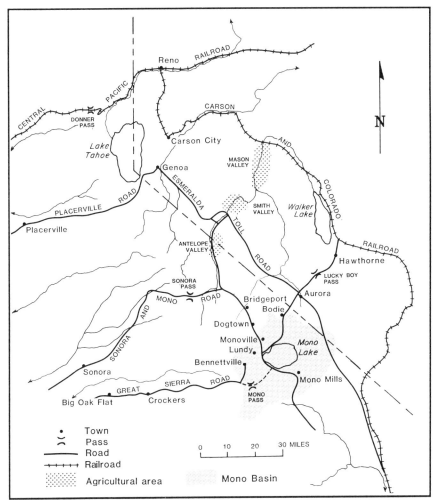

Figure 7. *Regional setting of Mono Basin, circa 1882. Based on map in Kersten, 1964.*

The only reason why placer diggings of such considerable extent and value have not already been worked, is the want of water sufficient for the process off sluicing; a project is now on foot for bringing the water of Cotton Wood Creek, distant about two miles, at an elevation by mechanical power of seven hundred feet, for the purpose of washing these deposits.[4]

Although this diversion of Cottonwood Creek from Mono into Walker Basin never took place, the proposal gives a measure of the Empire Company's initial ambition.

In his report, Silliman also discussed Bodie's other critical supply problem, that of wood. Since no trees grew near Bodie, wood for fuel, timbers for shoring the mines, and lumber for construction would all have to be freighted in from some distance. Silliman noted stands of pinyon pine, which was suitable for firewood, in three locations, all of which had been exploited to some extent by the Empire Company's predecessors: one in Bodie Canyon some five miles north of Bodie near Sunshine Valley; a second on the slopes above Trench Canyon about five miles east of the mining camp; and a third in nearby Cottonwood Canyon and its tributary ravines, three to four miles away.

Wood for lumber presented a greater problem. Forests about 20 miles away on the Sierran flank above Big Meadows (Bridgeport Valley) were the main source of Bodie's supply, and were to remain so for many years. Silliman, however, felt that they were inadequate to meet future needs, and suggested an alternative:

> Looking to the future wants of a great enterprise, such as is contemplated in the development of Bodie Bluff Mountain, it is interesting to know that there exists on the other side of Mono Lake, at a distance of about thirty miles, a large body of excellent pine timber, suited to all purposes of building and mining, with water sufficient to supply steam mills for its manufacture.[5]

It was not until 1881, long after the demise of the Empire Company, that this extensive forest of Jeffrey pine began to be exploited.

But Silliman could be cautious as well as ambitious. He warned the owners of the Empire Company that success depended upon adequate exploration. He reported that fourteen to fifteen hundred feet of shafts had been sunk upon various veins, but that "none of these are of adequate dimensions, or proper construction for an extensive and permanent extraction of ore."[6] All hoisting of ore out of the shafts had been done by hand windlasses, which would have to be replaced by steam hoisting works. But, advised Silliman, before extraction of ore was begun, more exploration was necessary. In his words, the success of the company

> depends on the fidelity with which those in charge of the enterprise adhere to the principle of keeping the work of exploration well in advance of the work of extraction.[7]

The Empire Company poured money into Bodie in 1864, erecting a boarding-house for its miners, a steam-operated stamp-mill to crush ore, a blacksmith's shop, hoisting works and a piped-water system. The costs of operation, including wages, were very high, due to Bodie's distance from sources of supply. With such costs, the ore had to be very rich to bring a profit. Rock assaying at $50 per ton in gold, usually considered very high-grade, did not pay to mine and mill at Bodie in these early years.[8]

High costs notwithstanding, the future looked bright to the Bodie miners in 1864. J. Ross Browne, who toured the mines in that year, has left us a detailed description of the fledgling town:

> At the head of Bodie Valley...is a beautiful natural location for a town... There are now some fifteen or twenty small frame and adobe houses erected for the use of the workmen; a boarding-house is already established; lots and streets are laid out by means of stakes; new houses are springing up in every direction, and speculation in real estate is quite the fashion. Groups of speculators were constantly engaged in examining choice locations, and descanting upon the brilliant future of the embryo city. A pair of boots, I suppose, would have secured the right to a tolerably good lot; but having only one pair, and that pretty well worn, I did not venture upon an investment.[9]

Browne, a knowledgeable observer of mining enterprises, did not predict success for the Empire Company; large companies like the Empire usually failed sooner or later, primarily because of the need for a very high rate of return:

> Whether or not the Bodie mines will be worked profitably on a large scale depends very much upon the system of operations introduced by the owners. As a general rule, large companies are less successful in the workings of mines than small parties and private individuals. The cause of this may be found in the fact that mining, like any other business, requires judicious and economical management, and strict personal attention, to be permanently profitable. Indeed the risks are so much greater than in any other business, that those maxims of economy and accountability which apply to the ordinary transactions of life possess still greater force as applied to the business of mining. Unnecessarily expensive mills, a loose system of disbursement, incompetent managers, and inefficient experts, have effected the ruin of many mines and many stockholders... Exorbitant and unreasonable demands for high dividends have been a fruitful source of failure. Capitalists are not satisfied unless they receive from two to five percent a month upon their investments; and superintendents work under a heavy pressure, and assume great hazards to produce that result... [But] permanency and extraordinary dividends are incompatible. Where the yield is evidently reliable, a reasonable percentage, regularly paid, is better than a larger amount which must necessarily involve greater risk and increased expenditure.[10]

In 1868 the Empire Company collapsed, having expended all of its capital, possibly as much as $500,000.[11] Silliman's warning that exploratory work should precede extraction of ore had not been heeded. From the first the company concentrated on milling the ores at hand, hoping that they would pay for later exploration. But the ores were not rich enough to produce the required rate of return and, as Browne had foreseen, the Empire Company failed. Bodie's truly rich lodes were yet to be discovered.

With the collapse of the Empire Company, individual miners again claimed the ground. Some joined together to form small cooperative companies. From 1868 until 1876 they explored with little fanfare and little reward. These years comprised Bodie's "quiet period." The population was tiny—voting records show an average of twenty votes cast at Bodie in Mono County elections between 1860 and 1877.[12] Bodie's fortunes reached their nadir in 1874, when the Empire stamp-mill, which had cost thousands of dollars to build, was sold for $450 in unpaid taxes.[13]

In this same year, however, Louis Lockberg and Peter Eshington made an important ore discovery. They acquired the old Bunker Hill-Bullion property, which had been located in 1861.[14] Soon after they took possession, a cave-in exposed a rich body of ore. For the next two years Lockberg and Eshington made a nice profit from the new lode, crushing the ore in water-powered arrastras on Rough Creek north of Bodie (an arrastra was a simple, cheap dragstone mill used to pulverize ore; it required a minimum of iron components and operated on mule power).[15] In September, 1876, three mining capitalists from San Francisco bought the promising mine for $75,000 and formed a new company, the Standard.[16] In its first year of operation, 1877, the Standard Company paid for the mine, erected its own stamp-mill, boarding-house and office, covered the cost of all expenses and supplies, and even declared four dividends to its stockholders totalling $200,000.[17]

Miners and capitalists responded quickly to the Standard Mine's success. The rush to Bodie began in the summer of 1877, and picked up momentum through the fall. Old buildings were moved from Aurora and Bridgeport, and new ones built at a fast pace.[18] By November there were three general stores, 12 saloons, six restaurants, a tinsmith, a shoemaker, a newspaper and a post office.[19] People arrived daily, looking for work in the mines, which they found, and shelter, which was more elusive.[20]

Wood was in critically short supply and very expensive. On November 14, the *Bodie Weekly Standard* reported:

The great cry in Bodie just now is wood! Everybody is asking his neighbor, 'What are we going to do for wood?' Teams are hauling in as fast as possible, and still there is a limited supply for our rapidly increasing population.

As the sawmills at Bridgeport were unable to meet Bodie's huge and sudden demand, lumber had to be freighted in from Adobe Meadows, 45 miles away, and even from Carson City.[21]

As the winter of 1877-1878 approached and people continued to arrive, shelter became harder and harder to find.[22] Although the Bodie newspapers warned people not to come until spring, the rate of new arrivals remained high; during late January, 1878, at the height of winter, 15 to 25 people arrived each day.[23] In early February Bodie's population had reached 1,400, with 50 families and 600 single men scrambling for lodgings.[24] Thirty saloons were doing brisk business, and 20 mines were in operation on Bodie Bluff and neighboring hills.

The most important source of information on Bodie during this boom period is a promotional pamphlet published in San Francisco in May, 1878, by a mining expert named Joseph Wasson: *Bodie and Esmeralda: An Account of the Important Revival of Mining Interest in the Bodie and Esmeralda Districts.* Wasson had come to Bodie the year before and watched it grow from tiny camp to boom town:

It is a wooden town, and in itself contains about 250 structures, some very presentable ones. About the mines proper there are about one hundred additional habitations and shelters of one kind and another.[25]

By the beginning of the summer of 1878, the population had risen to 2,000. Many were unable to find work. The employed miners organized a union and commanded $4 per day, a high wage.[26]

In *Bodie and Esmeralda*, Wasson described all the working mines individually. At that time, the spring of 1878, only the Standard Mine had found rich ore, but more than 20 other companies, some large, some small, were exploring Bodie Bluff and neighboring hills. Wasson predicted that the Bodie Company, which owned ground adjacent to the Standard Mine, would succeed in locating the continuation of the rich Standard lode into its own property. He was right; in the summer of 1878, a few months after Wasson's pamphlet had gone to press, the Bodie Company struck the rich vein, touching off furious stock speculation in San Francisco and turning the rush to Bodie into a mad dash. In just one month, August 1878, the Bodie Mine produced $600,000 in gold and silver bullion—an average daily output of almost $20,000. Bodie

Company stock jumped from 50 cents to $54 a share in just a few weeks, and the company paid its stockholders huge and unexpected dividends of $5 to $7 a share.[27] By December, 1878, the town's population had risen to 5,000, of whom only about 2,000 were able to find work in the mines.[28] Traffic of all kinds crowded the roads into Bodie from Sonora, Bridgeport and Carson City. In December, an observer at Mormon Station on the Big Meadows-Bodie Road sent the following report to a Bodie newspaper:

> There passes here daily about 60,000 feet of lumber; about fifteen loads of freight; twelve to fifteen loads of fruit and vegetables; and in addition...quite a number of teams daily pass here, loaded with chickens, turkeys, geese, ducks, and pigs, and with all kinds of household furniture, all on the way to Bodie.[29]

In an updated version of his pamphlet occasioned by the rich strike of the Bodie Company, Wasson described the mining situation he observed in late fall of 1878:

> Some twenty-odd steam hoisting works are now doing duty in the district, and among them all, old and new, at work in such a variety of places, the future of the district cannot remain undecided longer than the coming winter and early spring. The Summer of 1879 promises to be exceptionally lively and interesting.[30]

Before summer came, however, another winter had to be endured, and it proved to be harsh. Both firewood and lumber were extremely scarce. According to Grant Smith, who arrived at Bodie in 1879,

> the winter [of 1878-1879] found thousands of people poorly housed, poorly fed, with little employment, and with nothing to do but hang around saloons and gamble and fight and get drunk and lie out in the snow and die. Hundreds died that winter from exposure and disease, and nearly as many lost their lives by violence.[31]

When the spring of 1879 finally came, and routes into Bodie became passable again, mule and horse-drawn wagons rushed in vast amounts of supplies and building materials, mostly from Carson City, 110 miles distant. New arrivals, hoping to get rich, filled every stage-coach. Smith describes the scene he saw when he stepped off his stage:

> When I reached Bodie in June 1879, the terrors of the preceding winter had been forgotten, building was going on everywhere, new mines were being opened, new hoisting works erected, new mills being built, the excitement in mining stocks was at its height, nearly everybody had a mine or mining stock that would make him rich, and the region was in a delirium of excitement and activity. Gold and silver coin was as plentiful as nickels nowadays; all of the men about town appeared to have their pock-

Bodie in 1880. Courtesy, the California State Library.

ets full of money—and regally they spent it... The town was very poorly built up, and remained so; but one or two brick buildings were erected. The saloons and gambling halls and business houses, up and down the main street, were mere shacks, although sometimes very considerable in size. The boarding houses and lodging houses were of the flimsiest character and poorly heated except in the immediate vicinity of the stove; the homes of the miners and townspeople were built of rough boards, and very small, as a rule. Many people at first lived in tents and dugouts in the hillsides. Heating was difficult and inadequate; toilets were out-of-doors, reached in winter only by a trip through the snow; and the only lights were coal-oil lamps and candles. The only fuel was pine-nut wood; knotty and full of pitch and a most excellent fuel. There was no gas, no water except from wells and wagons, no coal, no hospitals, no nurses, no churches, no theaters, no entertainments of any sort except such as the people themselves devised.[32]

Wasson's prediction that the future of the district would be determined by developments during the first half of 1879 was prophetic. No new rich strikes were ever made; of the more than 20 mines being explored by tunnels running for thousands of feet in every likely direction, not one proved to be another Standard or Bodie. As 1879 wore on, it became clear that these two mines were the only big producers that Bodie was fated to know.

The vast majority ignored the truth. The population of the town peaked in 1880. The official census gave Bodie a population of 5,416, but it was probably somewhat higher, since many people complained that they had never been counted.[33] This figure is the highest for which there is reliable evidence.[34]

Over the next few years, as unprofitable mines were abandoned, the population of Bodie steadily declined. By the summer of 1883 it fell to about 2,500;[35] by September, 1888 to about 500,[36] supported almost entirely by the Standard Mine. Even the Bodie Company was unable to continue production on its own; in 1887 it merged with its rival the Standard Company. Between 1877 and 1888, all the mines at Bodie collectively produced $18 million in gold and silver bullion. Of this total the Bodie Mine contributed $4 million, and the Standard Mine $11 million; the Standard ranks as the ninth largest lode-gold producer in the history of California.[37]

Bodie as a Stimulus to Development in Mono Basin

The high cost of importing food and supplies from distant sources contributed to the miners' difficulties during the early years at Bodie and Aurora. The higher the costs of food and other necessities, the higher the cost of mining. In the early 1860s exceptionally rich ores were required to make the enterprise pay; others had to be ignored. As J. Ross Browne pointed out in 1864,

> Ores worth fifteen or twenty dollars a ton are necessarily cast aside, and only such as yield over thirty or forty dollars can be made to pay. There is always more poor ore in every mining district than rich; hence the preponderance of wealth is lost where the inferior ores can not be made available... It is to a general reduction of expenses, and not to the discovery of richer leads, that we must look.[38]

By the late 1870s, however, the situation had significantly improved. Settlers had established farms and ranches in suitable localities around Bodie. Good wagon roads linked it to Mono Lake (via Cottonwood Canyon), Bridgeport, Sonora, Adobe Meadows and Carson City. These developments lowered the price of food, wood and other supplies, which could now be produced locally. In addition technological advances allowed ores to be mined and milled at much lower costs. Lower-grade ores, present in greater abun-

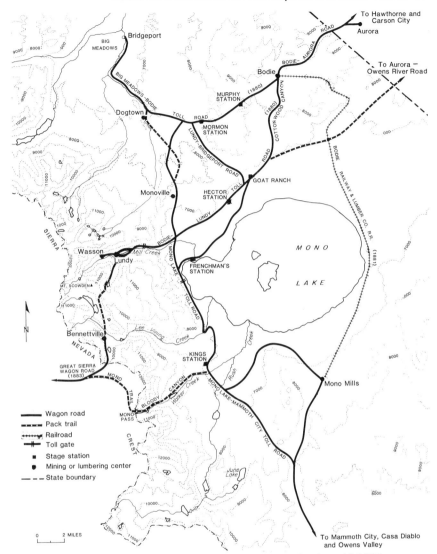

Figure 8. *Towns and transportation network in Mono Basin, mid-1880s.*

dance than rich ones, became increasingly profitable. The success of the Bodie mines in the late 1870s and early 1880s owed much to the gradual development of the region during the previous decade, the "quiet period."

The mining boom, however, transformed Bodie into the center upon which the surrounding area, and particularly the Mono Basin, depended. It became the source of inspiration and motivation for further developments, the provider of supplies from the outside world, and the locus of manpower, expertise and capital. The demands of Bodie and the abundant energy of the new arrivals, many of whom could not find work in the town itself, spurred the Mono Basin economy into a period of rapid development. Bodie stimulated not only prospecting and mining in the basin, but lumbering, homesteading, road-building, the construction of a railroad, the development of stage lines and stations and the founding of new towns as well—developments which are the subjects of the following sections.

Mining in Mono Basin

Conditions for the individual miner in Mono Basin had changed since the earlier days. During the Monoville activity (1857-1860), miners either worked for themselves or joined together in small organizations in which the work, the risks and the profits were shared equally. This was possible because placer mining required little capital; virtually anyone could set himself up with a pan, a rocker and a shovel. Vein mining, however, did not present such freedom to the individual miner. The high costs of construction of stamp-mills and hoists, and the drilling and blasting equipment needed for tunneling in hard rock, necessitated large amounts of capital which could only come from a mining corporation. Typically, the major investors lived in San Francisco or New York and rarely, if ever, visited the mines. The miner became an employee of the corporation and worked for a daily wage; he was not entitled to a percentage of the profits. By 1877, of course, these conditions had prevailed for many years west of the Sierra, in the Comstock, at Aurora and at Bodie, but in Mono Basin they were new.

The role of the prospector, however, had not changed. The individual who preferred to locate ore rather than work it still controlled his own destiny; he was no one's employee. His expertise lay in locating promising veins and selling his claims to the highest bidder, then moving on to the next find. The Bodie excitement brought a wave of new prospectors into the region, who fanned out in all directions. They soon made strikes in Mill Creek Canyon, where the town of Lundy would grow; on the steep slopes of Tioga Crest and Mt. Scowden above Lake Canyon, where the richest of all the Mono Basin mines, the May Lundy, would be developed; and along the crest of the Sierra Nevada, where, near present-day Tioga Pass, Bennettville would briefly struggle against the

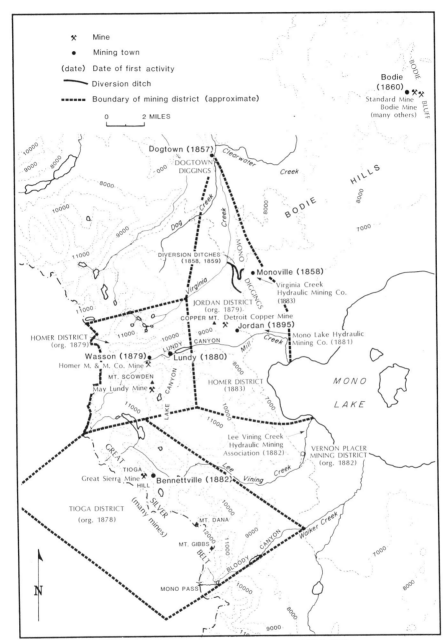

Figure 9. *Mines and mining districts in Mono Basin, 1880-1900.*

odds. It was not difficult for the discoverers of these claims to find buyers in Bodie, which abounded with entrepreneurs ready to take a risk.

Mining districts were quickly organized around the new strikes (Figure 9, page 55). In 1878 the Tioga District was formed, covering an area which extended for eight miles along the Sierran crest. In the next year, the Jordan District was organized, extending from the north shore of Mono Lake into Bridgeport basin and including the old Mono and Dogtown diggings; vein-mining as well as placering was now to receive attention. In 1879 the Homer District, the most successful of all the Mono Basin districts, was also organized. It included Tioga Crest, Lake Canyon and Lundy (Mill Creek) Canyon.

California miners had developed the institution of the mining district to provide a legal framework for resolving disputes over claims. Early in the life of a new mining camp the miners held a meeting to draw up a set of rules governing their claims. At the same time they established the boundaries of the new district to include existing claims as well as unclaimed ground which seemed likely to be of value.[39]

The man who discovered a specific mineral-bearing location had the exclusive right to exploit it, as long as he continued to do so. Normally a miner was allowed by district rules to hold only one claim by this process of "location," but he could increase his holdings by purchasing those of others. To avoid disputes and misunderstandings, the miners at their organizational meeting elected a District Recorder, whose duty was to maintain a descriptive list of all claims and to record all property transfers.[40]

If a district proved to be too large for the convenient transaction of all of its legal business—usually because new claims had been located away from the original district center—the dissatisfied miners could form a new district from the old by holding their own organizational meeting. The old district had no say in the matter, and could not prevent the division.

All three of the new Mono Basin districts—the Homer, the Tioga and the Jordan—depended largely upon Bodie as a source of supplies, men and expertise. Bodie was connected with the outside world (Figure 7, page 45). In 1879 roads linked the town with Bridgeport, Sonora and Carson City. By 1881, the Carson and Colorado Railroad had extended a line along the east shore of Walker Lake to Hawthorne, about 30 miles east of Bodie; heavy machinery could be shipped by rail to Hawthorne, and then taken by wagon road, via Aurora, to Bodie. The heavy freight wagons, drawn by teams of 20 horses or mules, could carry loads in excess of 20 tons.[41]

As mining in the new districts progressed, old roads were improved and new ones built. These early roads were all toll roads, each owned by a company or individual who had been granted an exclusive franchise by county authorities. In return for building and maintaining the road, the franchise-holder was entitled to collect tolls from all passing traffic. The toll rates, stipulated by the franchise contract, varied according to the nature of the traffic—stage coach, freight wagon, pack or saddle stock or domestic herd. The tolls were collected at toll gates located strategically along the roads.[42] Stage stations were usually associated with the toll houses. They furnished fresh horses for the stage-coach traffic, and food and lodging for passing travellers. The Bodie-Lundy Toll Road, built in 1880, boasted two stage stations, Hector Station and Goat Ranch (Figure 8, p. 53). Caesar Thiervierge built Frenchman's Station on the Mono Lake-Bodie Road (at the mouth of Mill Creek) in 1877; he had homesteaded the location, and then saw a profitable business opportunity as traffic increased. He operated a stable and an inn, and offered scenic excursions to Negit and Paoha islands.[43] King's Station at the foot of Bloody Canyon was the most northerly of the stations between Mono Lake and Mammoth City; Mike King erected buildings there early in the summer of 1880 and advertised "as fine and clean accommodations...as can be enjoyed at Bodie."[44] His location benefitted from the traffic up Bloody Canyon to the Tioga District mines, and was also well-suited to raising hay.

The toll roads and stations built between 1877 and 1880 enabled the Homer, Tioga and Jordan districts to communicate, without excessive difficulty, with Bodie and the world beyond. With the roads as a basis, a network of dependency developed between the various mining centers. Tioga miners descended to Lundy constantly for food, supplies and equipment, and Lundy relied equally upon Bodie. In a real sense, all the mining activity in Mono Basin depended upon the productivity of the Bodie mines, which enabled the town to be a relatively stable and long-lived regional mercantile center.

Lundy and the Homer District

Prior to 1879, when prospectors from Bodie scanned the slopes above Mill Creek for the first time, Lundy Canyon had been something of a backwater within Mono Basin. The narrow, densely forested valley floor was less attractive for settlement than the gentle open slopes and meadows around Mono

Lake. The forest in Lundy Canyon had been exploited for many years, however, beginning in the Dogtown and Monoville era. According to J. Ross Browne, a Mr. Lundy had settled on the north shore of the lake by 1864, and had erected a sawmill, undoubtedly on Mill Creek, to provide lumber for settlers[45]; perhaps he shipped some of the lumber to Aurora and Bodie as well. In 1876 W. O. Lundy began operating a water-powered sawmill equipped with a jig saw to cut lumber for Bodie, where things were just beginning to pick up.[46] The mill was located at the head of Lundy Lake; it may have been the same one mentioned by Browne.

During the summer of 1879, prospectors from Bodie located what they thought were rich placers along Mill Creek between Mono Lake and the mouth of Lundy Canyon.[47] The news of the discovery created some excitement, and

> a number of busy prospectors rushed to the new El Dorado. The placers did not amount to anything, and the prospectors began searching through the mountains, finding a region surpassingly rich in gold quartz. This was in August.[48]

The center of the new quartz discoveries lay on the south wall of Lundy Canyon about two miles upstream from Lundy Lake. Other quartz discoveries were made on the steep slopes above Lake Canyon.[49] Altogether about 40 men were at work in the area, which at that time was still part of Tioga District. Because the books and records of Tioga District were kept some distance away, the prospectors decided to organize their own local district.[50] On September 15, 1879, the Homer District was officially organized (Figure 9, page 55).[51]

The prospectors who located the first and best claims in the district—William Wasson (no relation to Joseph Wasson), L. L. Homer and C. H. Nye in Lundy Canyon, and O. J. Lundy in Lake Canyon—sold out to capitalists in San Francisco shortly after the organization of the district. From these transactions emerged two principal companies: the Homer Mill and Mining Company and the May Lundy Company. The Homer Mill and Mining Company started operations first, in October 1879, on the former claims of Wasson, Homer and Nye on the south side of Lundy Canyon upstream from Lundy Lake. The company property was 3,000 feet long by 1,200 feet wide, on the steep wall of the canyon where seven distinct quartz ledges ran parallel to one another, striking roughly north-south and dipping west.

The May Lundy Company's property was situated at an almost inaccessible spot high up on the east-facing slope of Mt. Scowden above Lake Canyon, at an elevation of over 11,000 feet. A 4,500 foot climb from Mill Creek made the mine especially difficult to supply and work; nevertheless, the May Lundy was to become the most successful mine in Homer District.

During the winter of 1879-1880, Bodie capitalists formed a third company, the Homer Land, Water, Mill and Mining Company. None of its 14 claims in Lundy and Lake Canyons[52] was destined to be very productive. In addition to these three large companies, individuals or partners located and worked many mines on low budgets. Jasper Parrett profitably operated the Parrett (or Parrot) Mine high on the south wall of Lundy Canyon for 29 years. He worked alone, using an arrastra to crush his ore.[53] The Jackson, the Lakeview and the Gorilla mines in Lake Canyon were other moderately productive small-scale operations.[54]

The mining companies of Homer District employed men at the same wage offered at Bodie. Skilled mechanics earned $5 a day, miners $4 and general laborers $3.50.[55] The developments in Homer District eased the unemployment problem at Bodie, where the fame of the Standard and the Bodie mines continued to attract more men than could possibly find work. Mining experts, too—engineers, surveyors, assayers and other professionals—found a new field for their services as Homer District developed.

All these mining operations created a new market for merchants, tradesmen and the farmers and ranchers around Mono Lake as well. The miners needed food, clothing, liquor, lodging, recreation, equipment and transportation. Almost as soon as the first strikes were made on the slopes above Mill Creek in 1879, two towns were founded on the valley floor to provide these things.

The towns, Wasson and Lundy, both vied for the miner's business. Wasson was founded first, at the site of William Wasson's homestead at Emigrant Flat next to the mines of the Homer Mill and Mining Company two miles upstream from Lundy Lake.[56]

Here quite a little camp is already [September, 1879] established, the wife and family of Wm. D. Wasson...lending an air of permanent settlement to the scene. About 25 miners and prospectors come and go from this neighborhood. Among the pioneers and more successful ones, are L. L. Homer (after whom the new district is named) and C. H. Nye.[57]

Wasson's growth was slow, in part because of the lack of a wagon road. A road had already been graded to the foot of Lundy Lake, but from there only a pack trail continued the two miles to Wasson.[58] By June 1880, when the Bodie and Mill Creek Toll Road finally reached it, Wasson consisted of about 20 log cabins and tents. During the next three years, while its rival downstream,

Lundy, grew and prospered, Wasson remained the small company town of the Homer Mill and Mining Company; it even came to be called Homer.

Lundy outshone Wasson primarily because of its better location; it was more easily reached by teamsters and traffic from Mono Lake, Bodie and beyond. Situated at the upper end of a handsome lake, it attracted settlers with the promise of pleasant views, boating, fishing and ice-skating. Most important, however, was its location near the mines in Lake Canyon, especially the rich May Lundy. The town had a virtual monopoly on business with this important section of Homer District, because it lay at the entryway of Lake Canyon.

The birth and early growth of Lundy is described in considerable detail in the first issue of its newspaper, the *Homer Mining Index*:

At the northwest end [of Lundy Lake] the canyon has widened out into a charming vale, perhaps three or four hundred acres in extent, which forms the townsite of the embryo city of Lundy... The townsite was once covered with a heavy growth of trees...but the prospectors and settlers have changed all this. The smaller trees have been cut down to build cabins, and the larger ones have fallen to the lumberman's ax. A sawmill on the shore of the lake converts their trunks into lumber... The multiplying houses among the stumps are evidences of their application to the wants of man. The willows have been chopped away here and here as obstructions and the whole scene now presents many of the aspects of the usual frontier clearing... The growth of Lundy has been remarkable. With the exception of a few log cabins, no building had ever been done prior to the first of last May [1880]. During that month upward of thirty frame houses, nearly all for business purposes, were built, besides a number of log houses. Two stores, selling general merchandise, seven saloons, two lodging-houses, several boarding-houses, two bakeries, a hotel, blacksmith-shop, assay office, butcher-shop, post office, express office, saw-mill, and a newspaper office—*The Mining Index*—are among the institutions of Lundy, and attest its rapid development.[59]

This first issue of the *Index* contains advertisements for many of these businesses. Three competing stage lines provided transportation between Lundy and Bodie, each sending out a coach from Lundy every other morning, returning from Bodie the next day, "rain or shine." The one-way trip averaged about five hours; the coaches travelled at a fast clip, changing horses at a number of stations along the way. The two general merchandise stores and three of the seven saloons were located on Main Street, which ran straight upcanyon from the head of Lundy Lake. The office of the *Homer Mining Index* was on the corner of B and Second streets; the paper came out every Saturday.

In June 1880 new arrivals at Lundy numbered between 15 and 20 per day. Work in the mines progressed rapidly with the summer weather; the May Lundy tunnel was extended 140 feet, and was lengthening at a rate of four feet per day.[60] At the end of June, the editor of the *Index* observed "houses...going up in all directions" around his office. The May Lundy Company established its offices on the corner of A and Main streets, and soon would open a well-stocked general store in town. With the optimism typical of new-born mining camps, the editor of the *Index* foresaw a time when "Mill Creek millionaires shall spit tobacco juice on the polished floors of Parisian saloons."[61]

By the spring of 1880 the Bodie and Mill Creek Toll Road had been graded out of the steep canyon wall north of Lundy Lake, following the old pack trail, and had reached the site of Lundy. At the end of June, surveys for a road into Lake Canyon were completed. The surveyed route extended from

> the east end of the lake to the mouth of Lake Canyon... The route affords the only approach to the canyon for teams, and the road is an imperative necessity if work on the mines is to be carried on.[62]

Construction was postponed until the beginning of November, when 25 men started work at the east end of Lundy Lake. A connecting road was built along the south shore to Lundy, so that teams descending from Lake Canyon would not have to go completely around the lake to reach the town. Severe winter conditions delayed completion of the Lake Canyon Toll Road itself until the following August.[63] The round-trip toll for one wagon drawn by a two-horse team was $1.50.[64]

As tunnels opened up veins and ore was extracted, the need for stamp-mills to crush the ore and separate the gold from the gangue became pressing. The smaller operations could get by with arrastras; two were constructed in Lake Canyon and one along Mill Creek, all driven by overshot water-wheels.[65] The May Lundy Company, however, needed a stamp-mill to handle its large quantities of ore, and began construction of a five-stamp mill at Lundy in August, 1880. The mill was completed and started operations in early October of that year, crushing the ore which the 65 miners of the May Lundy extracted at a rate of 25 tons per day.[66] Until the Lake Canyon Toll Road was finished the following summer, ore was packed down to Lundy by horses and mules; by mid-November, 1880, 1,200 tons had been transported to the mill in this laborious way.[67] The May Lundy Company owned another mill-site in Lake Canyon, but could not build a mill there, with the heavy machinery required, until the road up from Lundy was completed.[68] While the mill at Lundy may have been considered an interim measure, it was destined to be enlarged to 10 stamps and to remain the largest in Homer District until the 1890s.

Although it recognized that the mill was vital for the success of the May Lundy Company's operations, the local newspaper lamented the mill's effect on the lake's trout, a favorite local food. Everyone fished, including the Kuzedika, who speared and then sold the fish in town.

> The starting up of the May Lundy mill seals the doom of the trout in the creek and Lundy Lake... The slum and sediment is sure to kill them. It is a pity, but it cannot be helped, unless the mining companies would build a flume around the lake, which would cost several thousand dollars.[69]

Evidently the trout survived, however, as notes on local fishing continued to appear in the *Index* over the next few years, and fish still throve in the lake in the 1890s. These trout were not native to Mono Basin; they had either been intentionally introduced by the settlers, or had entered the Mill Creek drainage via the ditches built to divert Virginia Creek water to the Mono Diggings.[70]

Late in 1880, the problem of unemployment reared its head at Lundy, exacerbated by a lump in Bodie during the summer:

> Times are exceedingly dull in Bodie and money is scarce... Men unable to obtain employment have been leaving in numbers for the past six weeks; idle men are numerous.[71]

Many idle men came to Lundy hoping for work. Although the May Lundy Company's operations were continually expanding, the other companies in Homer District were not faring as well, and the May Lundy alone could employ only a fraction of the miners seeking work. On November 13 the *Index* made an unhappy note of the growing problem:

> Too many men [are] coming—the town is full of strangers. All night the saloons are crowded... More than one hundred men have come in here in the last two weeks. Most...are seeking employment, though some are looking around with a view to engaging in business. Every day there are batches of fresh arrivals. This influx...is to be regretted, for there are more men here now than can find work.

Despite unemployment, the merchants and businessmen of Lundy prospered during 1881 and 1882, as the mining companies continued to pour capital into Homer District. Lundy benefitted from developments in Tioga District as well; in 1882 it became the principal supplier of merchandise, mining equipment and services for the new town of Bennettville on Tioga Hill (see below, page 64). As the May Lundy mine proved to a rich producer of gold, the prospects for equal success in other mines seemed rosy; in January 1882 the editor of the *Index* wrote at length on "the approaching boom" in Homer District. In July, 1882 the May Lundy profitably employed between 50 and 60 miners. A little village sprang up in Lake Canyon just to supply their immediate wants; it boasted three saloons, two boarding-houses, and a laundry.[72] The population of Lundy at this high point has been estimated at near 500, a reasonable but unverifiable figure.[73]

The first indication that hard times were on the way was the failure of the Homer Mill and Mining Company in 1883. It had suspended operations at the approach of winter in 1882, and never started up again. In its three years of operations, the company had driven a tunnel 700 feet into the south wall of Lundy Canyon, and had run several crosscuts from the central tunnel to explore the numerous veins within its property. Its considerable labors, however, produced less than $200,000 in bullion, apparently not enough to make continued work worthwhile.[74] The failure of the Homer Mill and Mining Company tolled the death-knell for its company town, Wasson.[75]

Lundy weathered this collapse. The May Lundy and many other mines were still operating, and trade with Tioga District was considerable. Each week freight wagons hauled over 400 tons of ore down the Lake Canyon Toll Road to the stamp-mill at Lundy.[76]

The construction of the Great Sierra Wagon Road from the west side of the Sierra Nevada, which was actively underway in the summer of 1883, promised to reduce Lundy's isolation. The *Index* excitedly pointed out the benefits of the road, which was expected to be extended from Bennettville to Lake Canyon and link with the Lake Canyon Toll Road to Lundy early in 1884:

> Early next Spring, connection will be made between the May Lundy and the Great Sierra Wagon roads. This will give Mono county another outlet, a short-cut through Lundy and Tioga to railroad [sic], cheaper fares and freights, and at once open up one of the richest...mineral belts in the State... With a well-stocked stage-line on this road passengers from Bodie could be landed in San Francisco in twenty-four hours, and at little more than half the cost of the present mode of travel. Freight would also come at about half the time now required. The gap between the two roads is but four miles in length, and half of this distance would be easy and inexpensive grading.[77]

The *Index* even printed a wild "prediction" of "a population of 5,000 for Lundy...next summer."[78]

Such, however, was not to be the case. The Great Sierra Wagon Road was not extended to Lake Canyon; the mining concerns on Tioga Hill were having financial problems of their own. In May, 1884, although five more stamps were added to the May Lundy mill,[79] the end of the boom was just months away.

Early in the summer of 1884, the May Lundy Company could not pay its bills. In August the Mono County Sheriff closed the mine until such time as the company should pay off its creditors, mainly suppliers of merchandise in Lundy.[80] The miners who worked for the company were in debt as well, because they had not been paid for months and had been using local credit (backed by the good name of the May Lundy) for their purchases. For a few weeks it looked as if the company would make good on its debts and start operations again, but gradually the truth sank in: the May Lundy Company had failed.

During its four years of operations, the May Lundy produced the great bulk of the bullion from Homer District, though compared to the big mines at Bodie its production was not impressive. According to the California State Mineralogist's Annual Report for 1888, Homer District produced approximately $1 million between the fall of 1879 and 1888.

> About $837,000 of this amount, however, was produced from the May Lundy mine between October, 1880, and the suspension of operations by that company in the fall of 1884.[81]

The collapse of the May Lundy Company coincided with the failure of the Great Sierra Consolidated Silver Company at Bennettville. The two major props of Lundy's economy were both suddenly gone. Perhaps it is not a coincidence that the last extant issue of the *Homer Mining Index* from the 1880s is dated October 1, 1884. Henceforth, darkness wraps the hard period of Lundy's adjustment to depressed conditions.

Bennettville and the Tioga District

Although the Tioga District (Figures 9 and 10, pages 55 and 65) was not organized until 1878, the discovery of its principal vein occurred 20 years before. In 1859 a small party of miners left Monoville to return to the west side of the Sierra before winter set in. After ascending Bloody Canyon and crossing Mono Pass they explored the area around Tioga Pass and found a rich silver-bearing lode. Two members of the group, George Chase and Joshua Clayton, both from Sonora, returned the next year and laid claim to the location. They collected ore samples and took them to Monoville to be assayed. As they waited for the results, news of the great strikes at Esmeralda hit Monoville. Chase and

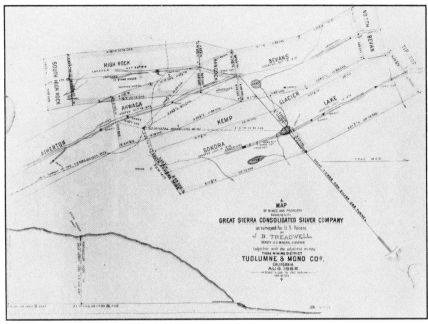

Figure 10. *Map of the Tioga Mining District, 1882. Courtesy, Yosemite National Park Research Library.*

Clayton, along with virtually everyone else, rushed to Aurora, never returning to work the lode they had found on Tioga Hill.[82]

The vein was relocated in 1874 by another man from Sonora, William Brusky, who named it the Sheepherder Lode. For four years he worked the claim alone while trying to convince wealthy Sonorans to take an active interest. He finally succeeded in 1878, when E. B. Burdick, Samuel Baker and W. J. Bevan organized the Tioga District.[83] The district centered upon the Sheepherder Lode and a newly discovered parallel vein nearby, the Great Sierra Lode, but extended over a large additional area along the Sierran crest from Mt. Conness to Mono Pass, and in an east-west direction from King's Station at the foot of Bloody Canyon to Lembert's Soda Springs in the Tuolumne Meadows (Figure 9, page 55).[84] During the next three years over 350 claims were located within Tioga District, most of them strung along the major vein system known as the Great Silver Belt, which ran from Tioga Hill south along the western slopes of Mts. Dana and Gibbs to Mono Pass.[85]

Many of the claims were initially owned and worked by men from Sonora. At first they relied upon Bodie for most of their supplies; in 1880, Lundy be-

Bennettville in 1896. Courtesy, Yosemite National Park Research Library.

came an alternative supply center. For food the Tioga miners depended on the settlers around Mono Lake:

> Mike King, of King's Ranch [King's Station], was in town... He don't have to hunt a market for his produce anymore, as the...Tioga District takes all his potatoes and vegetables.[86]

During the first few years, before a pack trail was built from Lake Canyon to Tioga Hill in 1881, the only practicable supply route was the Bloody Canyon trail. Under the heading "The Tioga Trade," the *Homer Mining Index* reported that

> Onofre Moreno, the well known Mexican packer, has entered into a contract with the Great Sierra Mining Company to pack 35 tons of freight from King's Ranch...up through Bloody Canyon and to the company's buildings on Tioga Hill. The freight will consist of provisions and machinery... Moreno left for Bodie on Wednesday to put twenty pack mules on the road.[87]

The Great Sierra Mining Company was the forerunner of the Great Sierra Consolidated Silver Company, a large corporation formed by a consortium of Eastern and Western capitalists. O. H. Brooks, a many-talented promoter from

Air compressor at the mouth of the Great Sierra Tunnel. Courtesy, Yosemite National Park Research Library.

Bodie who had supervised construction of a telegraph line to Lundy in 1880, became superintendent of the Great Sierra Mining Company in March, 1881. In April he travelled to Chicago and New York to spread word of the potential wealth of Tioga.[88] The result was the consolidation of all the claims on Tioga Hill; the Great Sierra Consolidated Silver Company bought up the existing companies—the Great Sierra Mining Company, the Mt. Dana Mining Company and the Consolidated Lake, Summit and Sonora Company. The complicated transactions, from which Mono County Judge Joseph Parker emerged as majority stockholder, were completed in November, 1881.[89]

The Great Sierra Consolidated Silver Company had ambitious plans. It deemed the tunnels which had already been started on the Sheepherder and Great Sierra Lodes useless. Instead it decided to cut a new tunnel, the Great Sierra, up into Tioga Hill from below the surface outcrops of the two veins. The tunnel would intersect the veins at depth, where the ores were expected to be richer than at the surface. Drifts and inclines would then be run along the strike and dip of the veins, facilitating large-scale extraction of ore. The plan had other advantages: because the tunnel approached the veins from below, gravity would assist water drainage and extraction of ore and waste-rock.

On paper the plan seemed excellent. Unfortunately, the rock at Tioga Hill was extremely hard. Every foot of tunnel had to be blasted and drilled, and the work turned out to be slow and costly. Moreover, the effort was being expended on waste-rock, not ore.

Nevertheless, the Great Sierra Consolidated Silver Company was confident and ambitious. It founded a company town a few hundred yards from the mouth of the Great Sierra Tunnel. In February, 1882, it was named Bennettville, after Thomas Bennett, president of the firm. The Bennettville post office opened on March 13, two days after the completion of a telephone line from Bennettville to Lundy (the poles are still visible crossing Tioga Crest into Lake Canyon). Here at Bennettville, at an elevation of nearly 10,000 feet, the company had its offices, a boarding-house for employees, several utility buildings, an assay office and a stable. The company promoted the site in the *Homer Mining Index*, where it was pronounced suitable for a city of 50,000 people.[90]

But the population of Bennettville remained tiny. The rigors of the location discouraged everyone but company employees. Transportation was very difficult, even though a pack trail had been extended from the terminus of the Lake Canyon Toll Road in 1881.

Before work on the Great Sierra Tunnel could begin, tons of blasting and drilling equipment had to be shipped in. The most direct route, from Lundy via Lake Canyon, seemed practicable—until it was tried. The Great Sierra Consolidated Silver Company shipped the equipment, totaling 16,000 pounds, from San Francisco to Bodie by railroad and freight-wagon, and from Bodie to Lundy on the Bodie and Mill Creek Toll Road. At the thousand-foot cliff above Lundy, the difficulties began. It took 12 men two months to haul the equipment from Lundy via Lake Canyon to Bennettville, a distance of about nine miles, in March and April, 1882, using specially made hardwood sleds. Without snow on the ground, the passage would have been impossible.[91]

Work on the Great Sierra tunnel began in earnest in May, 1882. It was designed as a double-track adit, that is, as an entry-tunnel with two steel tracks laid along its floor so that ore and waste-rock could be removed by cars. The tunnel was six feet wide by seven feet high; its length grew daily, but at a slow rate. Company engineers calculated that they would reach the Sheepherder Lode at a depth of 750 feet, and the Great Sierra at 830 feet. As work progressed through 1882 and 1883, it became clear that these estimates were much too low. Despite all the work done and money spent, the mine produced hardly a penny of silver during this time.[92]

In mid-1882 the Great Sierra Consolidated Silver Company embarked on a third ambitious project. Having started a tunnel and founded a town, it needed a decent road. The pack-trail from Lake Canyon had proven too difficult, and an easier route had to be found. The old Mono Trail that led west toward Yosemite was the obvious choice. During the fall of 1882, the company surveyed a route for the Great Sierra Wagon Road, beginning at Crocker's Station on the Big Oak Flat Road and more-or-less following the Mono Trail to Tioga Hill. The project fit in well with a larger scheme—construction of the California and Yosemite Short Line Railroad from Modesto to Mono Lake "via old Lee Vining Creek or McLean Pass."[93] The railroad company was incorporated in July, 1882, with $250,000 in working capital; these funds paid for surveying and constructing the Great Sierra Wagon Road.

Construction began at the end of April, 1883, and was finished early in September, at a total cost of $64,000. The length from Crocker's Station to Bennettville was 56 miles. At least 160 men, using only hand tools, advanced at an average rate of one-half mile per day.[94] The road was well-constructed and durable, later becoming the foundation for the modern Tioga Road.[95]

The road-builders intended to extend the road from Bennettville to Lundy, but this was never done. Nor was the California and Yosemite Short Line Railroad ever built. The Great Sierra Consolidated Silver Company was good at starting major projects, but poor at finishing them. By completing the Great Sierra Wagon Road as far as Bennettville, however, it did provide an easier supply route for the Tioga mines. Heavy equipment could be shipped from San Francisco to Copperopolis by rail, and then freighted in by wagon to Bennettville. The only further impediment to the progress of the Great Sierra Tunnel seemed to be the hardness of the rock.

The finances of the company, however, were not rock-solid. Hundreds of thousands of dollars had been spent with no return. To continue operations, the directors had repeatedly levied assessments on the company stock, and taken out large loans. The eastern stockholders accused the western ones of refusing to advance their portion of the money at critical times. In 1884 the situation became intolerable. Half the stockholders were taking all the risks, though all would benefit equally when the tunnel finally reached the Sheepherder Lode. The eastern directors finally decided to stop drilling, reorganize the company, and get rid of the "dead wood."[96]

On July 3, 1884, all operations shut down. The Great Sierra Tunnel had been driven 1,784 feet into the rock, but still had not reached the Sheepherder Lode. The buildings at Bennettville were boarded up and the miners laid off; the Bennettville post office closed in November. The Executive Committee of the Great Sierra Consolidated Silver Company planned to reorganize the company as soon as possible, but found itself unable to raise more working capital.[97] Three hundred thousand dollars had been spent; at best a few thousand dollars of silver had been produced.[98]

Thus, in 1884, at the same time that the fortunes of Homer District were sinking, the principal mine in Tioga District collapsed as well. Not until 1888 was the reorganization of the Great Sierra Consolidated Silver Company accomplished. In 1889, it drove the Great Sierra Tunnel to 2,000 feet, but the Sheepherder Lode proved as elusive as ever. Then the company folded for good.[99]

Jordan and Vernon Districts

As early as 1860, miners at Monoville had located some of the source veins for the rich gold placers in the Mono Diggings. According to a report by J. Ross Browne published in 1868, ore was extracted from these veins and crushed in arrastras driven by water diverted from Virginia Creek,

> and for a time good results were obtained; but the pay streak in these lodes was very narrow, rendering it expensive to get out sufficient ore to keep the arrastras running, which led to a final cessation of work upon them. With more thorough development it is thought these veins could still be worked with remunerative results.[100]

It was not until 1879 that the veins again received attention. In April of that year, the Jordan Mining District was organized. It centered on the old Mono Diggings and on Copper Mountain just north of Mill Creek. The exact boundaries of the district were defined in June, 1881 (Figure 9, page 55).[101]

In the summer of 1880, a handful of miners at the Mono Diggings were picking up where their predecessors of the early 1860s had left off:

> A number of very promising ledges have been located, and some work has been done...the ore is uniformly high-grade. Some parties have put up an arrastra... Old ditches, dug in early days by the placer miners, bring water into the diggings from Virginia Creek, and this water furnishes the power to run the arrastra.[102]

A year later hydraulic mining of gravels began both in the Mono Diggings and along lower Mill Creek. The Mono Lake Hydraulic Mining Company built a dam at the foot of Lundy Lake in December, 1881, evidently to regulate the flow of Mill Creek to provide an adequate supply of water for its hydraulic operations downstream through late summer and fall.[103] The company held patents to a total of 400 acres of gravels along Mill Creek just below the mouth of Lundy Canyon.[104] In the Mono Diggings, the first hydraulic mine, the Squawvine, began work in the late summer of 1881.[105] By the spring of 1883 a much larger enterprise, the Virginia Creek Hydraulic Mining Company, owned and worked 3,200 acres of gravel deposits there.[106] The company produced a total of $50,000 in gold between 1883 and 1888.[107]

The Jordan District contained, in addition to gold-bearing veins and placers, silver and copper lodes as well. Its most productive mine, the Detroit Copper Mine, was located on Copper Mountain northeast of Lundy Lake. Between 1879 and 1883, it produced about $60,000 of ingot copper, smelted in a small furnace constructed on the site.[108] This sum was an inadequate return on the capital invested, however, and the Detroit Copper Mining Company suspended work in 1883. The mine opened again in the 1890s and was worked intermittently until 1908 (see below, page 91).

In May, 1882, men intent on working lower Lee Vining Creek gravels organized the Vernon Placer Mining District.[109] The gravels, extending from about one to two miles above Mono Lake, had attracted attention as early as July, 1880, when several miners were working claims on the south bank.[110] By June 1882, 26 claims had been located, each 20 acres in extent.[111] Some of the miners organized the Lee Vining Creek Hydraulic Mining Association to work their adjacent claims cooperatively. Their plans included building a flume to bring water from upstream to work the gravels hydraulically.[112] What came of these plans is unknown, for there is a year-long hiatus in extant issues of the *Homer Mining Index* after the July 29, 1882 issue; later issues make no mention of further activities.

Lumbering in Mono Basin

Bodie and the neighboring mining districts created an almost insatiable demand for wood. The mines themselves required large quantities of squared timbers for shoring within the tunnels; surfaced boards, rough flooring and

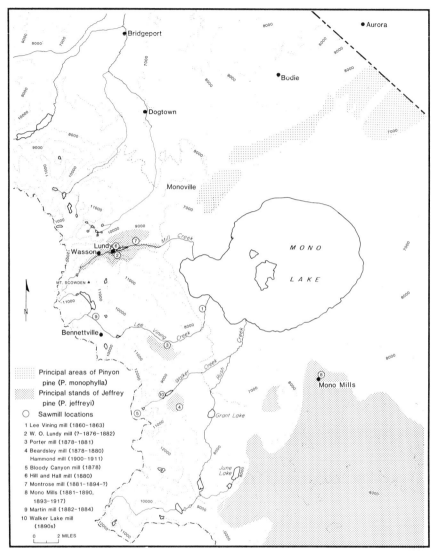

Figure 11. *Sawmills and principal timber stands in Mono Basin, 1860-1911.*

shingles were needed for building construction. The greatest demand of all was for cordwood; huge quantities were necessary to provide the steam power for the stamp-mills, hoisting works and drainage pumps associated with the mines. In addition, people needed vast amounts of cordwood simply to survive the cold winters; shortages led to considerable misery on more than one occasion.[113]

Bodie newspapers give an indication of the magnitude of the demand. As winter approached in late 1878, over 18,000 cords of pinyon pine lay stored in various locations waiting for the rise in price that would accompany the first severe cold spell.[114] The large mining companies had huge quantities stacked on their properties, and standing orders for more; the hoists, mills and pumps of a single large firm could consume as much as 24 cords of wood per day.[115] The Standard Company started the winter of 1878-79 with 9,000 cords piled in its yards.[116]

Pinyon pine, the principal fuel, grew in a number of places around Bodie on slopes between 7,000 and 8,000 feet. In Mono Basin the biggest stands were along the flank of the Bodie Hills overlooking Mono Lake, and on the slopes above Trench Canyon southeast of Bodie; additional small patches were scattered on slopes east, southeast and west of Mono Lake (Figure 11, page 72).

Pinyon pine, however, was also an extremely important food resource for the Kuzedika Paiute, who subsisted largely on pinenuts during the winter. The felling of the trees was catastrophic for the Kuzedika, not only because it deprived them of food, but also because they considered the trees sacred. According to John Muir, "it is the Indians' own tree, and many a white man have they killed for cutting it down."[117]

In 1877, when pinyon pines were suddenly subjected to large-scale cutting to supply the Bodie boom, the Kuzedika were greatly angered. They began to interfere with the wood-cutters, and some violence occurred. The November 7, 1877 issue of the *Bodie Weekly Standard* printed an article, "Paiutes on the Warpath," which describes one incident and sheds light on the attitudes of some, perhaps a majority, of the whites toward the Kuzedika:

Men chopping wood on the eastern side of Mono Lake, for the mining companies of Bodie, have been threatened by Paiute Indians in that vicinity, who swear by the "Great Father" that they will shoot every "white squaw" among them if they do not quit work, clear out and leave the aborigines in sole possession. What has given rise to this sentiment, people are at a loss to conceive, unless it be the chronic jealousy of the redskins on beholding the rapid growth of the white population, and contrasting the difference between their own debased condition with the continually increasing comforts and luxuries of the white settlers. If a little sense could be hammered into the clouded intellect of these red brothers and some of their chronic laziness thrashed out of them, they might some day be able to comprehend the laws of nature sufficiently and grow ambitious enough to induce them to work for a living like the rest of mankind, instead of frittering their time away in gambling and stretching their lazy carcasses in the sun's warm rays.

Old-growth Jeffrey pine logs at wood landing, Mono Mills, 1911 or 1912. Courtesy, the Mono Lake Committee Research Library.

It is to be hoped the threats of these worthless creatures may prove but idle talk, yet it will not do to let it pass and take no preventatives against an attempt at their fulfillment. Let all be on their guard, yet careful to do nothing calculated to arouse the drowsy creature who is growling in his sleep. Throw a biting dog a bone rather than a stone. Let this be the motto of all.

Teamsters brought wood into Bodie from near and far. In the late 1870s the Mono Basin supplied a large proportion of Bodie's wood, but a small part of its finished lumber. The bulk of the lumber was cut and milled at Bridgeport; some also came from Benton, Adobe Meadows and Carson City. As transportation costs were high, the mining companies soon took steps to exploit a more convenient, untapped source.

Mono Mills

In 1880 a consortium that included men from the more successful Bodie mining firms acquired the timber rights to a 12,000 acre portion of the large Jeffrey pine forest east of the Mono Craters.[118] The forest had been eyed by Bodie miners ever since Silliman's 1864 report pointed out its potential. In February 1881, the group formed the Bodie Railway and Lumber Company. By the middle of November they had constructed a narrow gauge railroad from Bodie Bluff to the forest (Figure 8, page 53). By cutting, milling and transporting their own lumber, they were able to deliver lumber to Bodie's mines at a greatly reduced price.[119]

The original plans called for the railroad to run along the west shore of Mono Lake so that Lundy could be supplied with wood as well.[120] The plan was changed, however, and the railroad was built along the east shore of the lake—a much shorter and less costly route. At its southern terminus, 32 rail-miles from Bodie, stood the company sawmill, which had been completed during the summer in time to turn out the ties for the railroad. In the first few years of operation the mill was known as Mono Saw Mill, and the small village which developed around it was simply called Mono. Later, the mill and village together were called Mono Mills (Figure 11, page 72).

Water for the steam-powered sawmill, the railroad engines and for domestic use was piped to Mono Mills from a spring located about five miles to the east.[121] Jeffrey pine logs were hauled from the forest to the mill by solid-wheeled logging trucks pulled by teams of as many as ten oxen.[122] The mill, large and modern for its day, had five saws capable of turning out 80,000 feet of lumber every ten hours.[123] Twenty-five men worked in the mill, and about 200 in the forest cutting and hauling timber.

In its first year of operation, 1882, the railroad delivered five million board feet of lumber and 27,000 cords of wood to Bodie at substantially lower prices than ever before. In 1879 and 1880, surfaced pine lumber cost $100 per thousand board feet; in 1882, the Bodie Railway and Lumber Company delivered the same amount for $30. In March, 1880, a cord of wood cost $20; cordwood from Mono Mills, produced from the tops, limbs and scraps of the pines felled for lumber, sold at first for $11, and later $8 per cord.

Jeffrey pine cordwood from Mono Mills reduced the demand for pinyon, but did not eliminate it entirely. The nut pine was full of pitch and burned very hot, making it a desirable fuel. In addition, most of the pinyon was cut and teamed by Chinese, who were willing to work at a lower profit than white wood-cutters and teamsters. The Chinese thus continued to supply nut pine cordwood at competitive prices even after Mono Mills was in full operation. Many of the smaller white-owned wood and lumber firms, however, were driven out of business by the new company.[124]

Bringing fuel wood to the Mono Mills railhead, 1911 or 1912. Courtesy, the Mono Lake Committee Research Library.

Mono Mills and the skidway to the railroad tracks, date unknown. Courtesy the Mono Lake Committee Research Library.

The "Mono" engine on its way to Bodie, date unknown. Courtesy, Mono Lake Committee Research Library.

The Bodie Railway and Lumber Company soon realized that the lumber business was dependent on the laws of supply and demand. The company had continued logging and milling operations through most of the winter of 1881-1882 and the spring as well, to build up a supply for the summer. But it found, in June 1882, that it had created a glut of wood that temporarily depressed the market:

> The town of Mono, about the sawmills of the Bodie Railway and Lumber Company, is rather dull at present, on account of the temporary suspension of operations occasioned by a glut in the lumber and wood market of Bodie. A few Chinamen are still engaged in chopping wood, which Hank Martin's teams are hauling to the railroad track, and Sprague Chase and his employees are still hauling logs to the sawmill, but outside of these and the train men the white men of the camp are idle. Considerably more than 1,000,000 feet of lumber was shipped to Bodie during the past month, besides vast quantities of wood.[125]

"The town of Mono" consisted of various company buildings besides the mill—a round house for the locomotives, a machine shop, blacksmith's shop, boarding-house and a commissary with a saloon. By October, 1882, a village had grown up that contained, along with the company buildings, about 30 small houses, a second boarding-house and two general stores.[126] In addition to whites and Chinese, Kuzedika men worked in the forest and on the railroad, where they maintained the track—a job that others avoided because of the extreme summer heat along the east shore of Mono Lake. The Kuzedika lived at Mono Mills during the summer; they were considered excellent workers.[127]

Business at Mono Mills rose and fell with the fluctuating fortunes of the Bodie mines. A little lumber and wood was sold in Aurora and to mines in the Masonic District northwest of Bodie, also a variable market. Bodie was prosperous through the fall of 1882, with many of the smaller mines active along with the large ones. In November, 1882, however, two important mines—the Noonday and the Redcloud—suddenly failed. Other mines followed in 1883; the population of Bodie fell to 2,500 as many discouraged people moved on. Bullion production from Bodie declined between 1885 and 1887 to about $500,000 per year, one-sixth of the annual yield of the peak years, 1878-1881. In 1888, production fell to a paltry $126,000, almost all from the Standard Mine; the population of Bodie was down to less than 500.[128] The rapid decline of the Bodie mines forced a total suspension of cutting and milling at Mono Mills in 1890, and the mill remained idle for three years.[129]

A resurgence of activity at Bodie opened Mono Mills again in 1893, and it operated continuously until 1917, but on a much smaller scale. From 1895 to 1903 the average annual cut was about 500,000 board feet, one-tenth of the 1882 output. The working season was confined to one six- to nine-week period in the summer. Shoring timbers made up 75 percent of the mill product, while surfaced boards accounted for only 25 percent, an indication that little building was going on at Bodie during this period. The yearly demand for fuel wood had also declined markedly from former levels; 1,500 to 2,000 cords sufficed to augment the new hydro-electric power supply.[130]

In 1904 a Forest Service inspector, W. A. Langille, visited Mono Basin to assess the suitability of its forests for addition to the Sierra Forest Reserve. His two reports provide the only detailed information on timber-cutting activity at the turn of the century.[131] According to Langille, the Bodie Railway and Lumber Company paid taxes on 14,796 acres of timberland and 720 acres of cut-over land (to hold onto the right-of-way for the railroad) in 1904. The company had stopped paying taxes on 4,500 acres of cut-over land, allowing it to revert to state ownership. Langille estimated that these 4,500 acres had yielded an average of 5,000 board feet of mining timbers and lumber and 15 cords of wood per acre.[132] The total cut from this abandoned land was thus approximately 22.5 million board feet of timbers and lumber and 67,500 cords of wood.

From 1904 to 1912, the demand for all types of wood products declined. Although a brief revival at Aurora between 1912 and 1916 stimulated business at Mono Mills, both mill and railroad shut down forever in 1917. In 1918 the mill was dismantled and the railroad tracks removed and sold to pay off the company's debt.[133] The ties, however, the first products of Mono Mills, still lie in place along the east shore of Mono Lake.

Small-scale Lumbering Operations

Relatively little information exists on the numerous small sawmill operations that sprang up here and there in Mono Basin for brief periods (Figure 10, page 65). The first mills, built to supply the miners at Monoville with lumber for buildings and flumes, were probably established on the slopes below Mt. Dunderberg and along Mill Creek. In 1864, J. Ross Browne observed a sawmill, probably on lower Mill Creek, that supplied building materials for settlers around Mono Lake.[134] Lee Vining is known to have erected a sawmill somewhere along Lee Vining Creek by 1861; Clayton's 1861 Map of Esmeralda and Mono (Figure 6, page 28) shows the probable site, "Vining's Rancho," about halfway between Mono Lake and the present town of Lee Vining. Few Jeffrey pines grow there today, but "it is likely that early cutting depleted a denser stand."[135] Vining freighted lumber to Aurora, which was then at its height.

During the "quiet period" in Mono Basin the demand for lumber was low. Sometime before 1876, W. O. Lundy built a water-powered jig-saw mill on Mill Creek at the head of Lundy Lake capable of producing about 1,500 board feet per day.[136] He cut from stands of pine along the valley bottom.[137] This small production met the demands of the slow but steady influx of settlers to the north and west shores of Mono Lake, and Lundy sold lumber at Bodie as well.[138]

In the late 1870s, developments at Bodie and in the Homer and Tioga districts stimulated other entrepreneurs to build sawmills in Mono Basin. The G. L. Porter Company of Bodie constructed the Porter Mill on Lee Vining Creek in 1878 (Figure 11, page 72).[139] Its steam-powered circular saw could turn out 25,000 board feet of lumber per day, over 15 times the capacity of Lundy's mill.[140] The logs were cut from a sizeable mixed conifer forest on the south flank of Lee Vining Canyon. In 1904 the stand still contained an estimated 3,960,000 board feet of merchantable timber.[141]

The Porter Company's primary market was Bodie, where it maintained a lumber yard. The long haul was shortened in 1880, when the company constructed at least two barges and contracted with the owner of a steamboat, the

Rocket, to tow the barges across Mono Lake from the mouth of Lee Vining Creek to Warford Springs on the north shore. Notes on the Porter Company's flotilla appeared in Mammoth City and Bodie newspapers:

> A flat boat belonging to Porter Co. was wrecked a few days ago on Mono Lake by wind. A new one is being built.[142]

> J. L. Porter and Co. will soon have a passenger steamer on Mono Lake for use in towing barges of lumber across the lake from their mills in Lee Vining Creek, thence by road from the east end of the lake to Bodie.[143]

The *Rocket*, built in San Francisco, had plied the Bay for only a few months when J. S. Cain of Bodie bought it in 1879. The vessel weighed over five tons; even dismantled, its pieces made heavy loads for the wagon teams that hauled it to Mono Lake from the railhead at Carson City. After towing the Porter Company's lumber barges for over a year, the *Rocket* was purchased by the Bodie Railway and Lumber Company in 1881 to haul rails, locomotives, cars and sawmill equipment across the lake during the construction of the railroad and Mono Mills. In 1882 and 1883, the *Rocket* was employed by Israel Russell's U. S. Geological Survey party. In 1888, storm winds wrecked the steamer on the lake's east shore; its machinery was stripped and taken to the Mono Mills machine shop for parts.[144]

Bodie was not the sole market for the Porter mill. The mines of Homer District were developing faster than the Mill Creek mills could supply them. In September, 1880,

> Manager Pike, of the May Lundy [Mine], went to Porter and Company's mills on Lee Vining Creek...to make arrangements for lumber needed by the company for the erection of new buildings.[145]

Approximately 200 acres of the Lee Vining Creek pine forest were cut by the Porter Company before its demise in 1881.[146] With the completion of the Bodie Railroad and the much larger and modern Mono Mills, the Porter Company found itself out-produced and undersold. In 1882, a Bridgeport lumber firm purchased and removed the hardware of the Porter mill.[147] Its total output had been, at a minimum, one million board feet, and perhaps twice that.[148]

With the rush into Homer District in 1880, W. O. Lundy soon found that his lumber business had local competition, a fact which gave him no pleasure:

> Hill and Hall of Lundy are cutting 15,000 feet of lumber per day. Customers are packing lumber from the mill as fast as sawn, $40.00 per 1,000 feet. Mr. Lundy proposes to get out an injunction.[149]

Hill and Hall's water-powered circular-saw mill at Lundy operated for less than one year. Most of the lumber went to Bodie, even though demand at the Lundy and Homer mines outstripped supplies throughout that year.[150]

After the pine stands along lower and middle Mill Creek were exhausted, cutting continued on the slopes above. A third mill was erected, the Montrose, on the flank of Copper Mountain (Figure 11, page 72).[151] The Montrose mill operated successfully through the 1880s; the *Homer Mining Index* carried advertisements for Montrose lumber in 1894.[512]

Demand for lumber at Lundy and in the Homer mines was intense from 1880 to 1882, but declined in the next two years as the larger mines closed. After 1884, lumbering, like mining, was sporadic. It is impossible to estimate total production of the Mill Creek sawmills, but in the valley bottom timber was almost completely eliminated, and the stands on the slopes above were significantly thinned out. Due to second growth, however, Lundy Canyon probably appears much the same today as it did originally.

Developments on Tioga Hill led to the erection of a sawmill on upper Lee Vining Creek in 1882.[153] Owned and operated by John Martin, the mill was situated just downstream from Saddlebag Lake, about one mile from Bennettville and the Great Sierra Tunnel (Figure 11, page 72). Its circular saw was steam-powered—the boiler had been hauled up over the snow from Lundy— and could turn out 3,000 board feet per day of lodgepole pine.[154] The lumber was delivered to Bennettville under a contract with the Great Sierra Consolidated Silver Company. Needless to say, when the mining operations ceased in 1884, so did the lumber operations.

The Beardsley sawmill was built on a tributary of Parker Creek in 1878 to supply timbers for Bodie and lumber for nearby settlers (Figure 11, page 72). Located in a small mixed pine forest dominated by Jeffrey pine, it had a steam-powered circular saw capable of cutting 10,000 board feet per day.[155] When it shut down in 1880, only a fraction of the timber had been cut. In 1900 the Hammond Mill began operations on the same location; J. P. Hammond had acquired the timber patent for 160 acres of the pine forest, which included the best remaining stand. He ran his mill for 30 to 40 days each summer through 1911, using horses to haul the logs out of the steep forest to the mill along 700 yards of chute. The mill cut 400,000 feet of lumber in the 1902 and 1903 seasons; by 1904 it had milled 40 to 50 percent of the available timber.[156] The exhaustion of usable timber and a depressed market probably caused the mill's closure in 1911.

Two other sawmills existed for short periods in Bloody Canyon. The miners of the Golden Crown and Ella Bloss mines built a small, portable mill near Mono Pass in 1878 to supply their immediate needs. It was removed in 1878 or 1879 and packed into lower Mono Basin.[157] The second sawmill, which operated at Walker Lake in the 1890s, probably exploited the Jeffrey pines growing on the large moraines confining the lake.[158]

Agriculture and Grazing in Mono Basin

The boom at Bodie stimulated agriculture in the Mono Basin, just as it had mining and lumbering. Bodie provided a ready market for the surplus food produced by the settlers around Mono Lake; so too did Lundy, Wasson, Bennettville and Mono Mills. These markets brought "good times" to the basin's farmers, who could now convert surplus hay, grains, vegetables, meat and dairy products into money to buy previously unobtainable or scarce goods and luxuries. The success of the mines was thus critically important to the settlers.

The Bodie excitement also led to the establishment of many new farms in the basin. Some of Bodie's gold-seekers quickly abandoned their quest. Work in the mines, if it could be found, was hard and not always profitable. Many miners had been farmers before; for some, the virgin land around Mono Lake presented an attractive alternative to working deep in dark tunnels. In addition, word spread across the country that good farm land lay nearby for the settler. Margaret Currie Calhoun, in her valuable account *Pioneers of Mono Basin*, explains how her mother and father, Anna and Charles Currie, were induced to leave their home in Marshall, Minnesota in 1885 to come to Mono Lake. They had received letter after letter from their relatives:

> The Wilsons wrote them often of the wonderful climate at Mono Lake, and begged them to come... So one day in October 1885, as Anna sat reading a letter to her husband from the Wilsons in which they were urging them to come, she...said, 'Shall we go?'... By November the home was sold.[159]

Other families came from even greater distances. The DeChambeaus were French Canadians who came to Bodie in 1878 and 1880, and settled in Mono Basin.[160] A group of Italian families left their mother country intending to settle at Genoa, Nevada, but upon arrival found it overcrowded. Hearing of good,

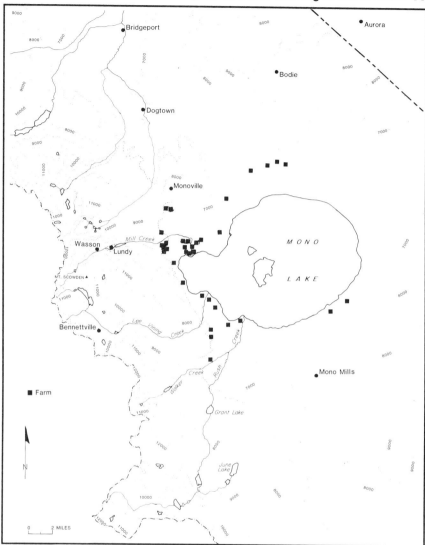

Figure 12. *Farm concentrations in Mono Basin, 1880-1900.*

open land at Mono Lake, they established a string of homesteads along the north shore by 1882.[161]

For poor Americans and for immigrants, Mono Basin in the 1880s was still a frontier where virgin land could be had at little or no cost. Under the Homestead Act of 1862, up to 160 acres could be acquired free. The settler, after making application at the local land office (located in Bodie after 1878), had only to live on and cultivate the land for five years to become its owner. Under the Desert Land Act of 1877, the settler could obtain a parcel of up to 640 acres of "dry land" by filing a declaration of intent to irrigate it within three years, and by paying 25 cents per acre.[162]

Agricultural settlement seems to have been most active between 1878 and 1882, when the mines were at peak production. As an early issue of the *Homer Mining Index* reported in August, 1880:

There are many fine farms along the shores of the lake, and the area of cultivation is increasing rapidly. More than 2,000 acres of virgin soil were put under the plow last spring and next year a much greater area will be reclaimed.[163]

Two years later, the area of cultivated land was still increasing rapidly:

The area of land under cultivation around Mono Lake has been greatly increased— nearly doubled, in fact—the present season, and the farmers are assured of abundant crops. The grain fields are clothed in green, green corn is putting forth its fifth and sixth blades, and vegetables are springing up as if by magic. Owing to the late and unusually heavy snowfall of the past winter, water is abundant in every gulch, and all the newly cleared sagebrush land is being freely irrigated.[164]

The "reclamation" of the land was an arduous process, described in detail by Calhoun:

Nearly all the Currie property was covered with sagebrush which had to be broken down and then grubbed out. Father first built a drag out of two large planks, nailed together with large spikes protruding on the underside. These planks were pulled over the sagebrush covered ground by two horses with the driver following. This contrivance broke and tore the brush as it went along. Any brush remaining, after the dragging, had to be dug out by hand. The sagebrush was then stacked into piles and burned. The land was now ready to be ploughed with a hand plough, drawn by two horses... Farmers would often follow the plough all day long. When a piece of ground was ploughed, it next had be leveled with a Fresno or Slip Scraper drawn by two horses. The field was then fertilized with cow manure and watered. After all this was done, the seed was scattered by hand from a canvas bag hanging from the farmer's neck. This method of farming was followed by all the farmers at Mono.[165]

Because the pumiceous, sandy soil of the newly-converted land was very porous, it required large amounts of irrigation water to raise crops; access to a water supply lasting through most of the summer was a necessity. As a result most of the farms were clustered along the lower reaches of the streams draining the Sierra Nevada. Approximately 15 were concentrated along Mill Creek below Lundy Canyon during the 1880s and 1890s (Figure 12, page 83).[166]

Haystack, barn and field at the Mattly Ranch between lower Lee Vining and Rush creeks, date unknown. Courtesy, Robert C. Calhoun.

Hay wagons entering Bodie, date unknown. Courtesy, Robert C. Calhoun.

About ten homesteads developed on lower Lee Vining, Walker and Rush creeks and along the Mono Lake shoreline between the deltas of Rush and Lee Vining creeks. Isolated ranches were established at various springs around the lake, especially along the north shore at the foot of Bodie Hills. Caesar Thiervierge of Frenchman's Station, called "Fisher" by his neighbors, selected a spot on Paoha Island, as noted in the *Index*:

> Fisher, the French rancher, has a large number of chickens and rabbits on his new ranch on the large island in Mono Lake, and both are multiplying rapidly. He has abandoned the solfatara hatchery, as the chickens hatched by the steam from the vol-

canic vents on the island are not hardy. His rabbits keep fat on alfalfa, which is already in bloom on the island. The chickens keep as fat as they can roll, without being fed, and their eggs are beauties... Mr. Fisher is now engaged in sowing grain and preparing a vegetable garden at his island home.[167]

Water was diverted from streams and springs by open ditches controlled by sluices. In the favored localities selected by the homesteaders, water was plentiful and the soil moderately fertile. The growing season, however, was short, averaging about 110 frost-free days per year, and untimely frost was always a danger. A heavy winter, especially one in which snow continued to fall into May or even June, could cut the growing season very short indeed.

Irrigated land in the Mono Basin during the 1880s and 1890s probably totalled about 4,000 acres. This estimate derives from S. T. Harding's unpublished manuscript, "Water Supply of Mono Lake Based on it Past Fluctuations:"

The census of 1919 reported 4,190 acres irrigated from the tributaries of Mono Lake. In 1929 the census reports 11,500 acres as irrigated. The increase form 1919 was mainly in the areas of the Cain Irrigation Company on pumice soil growing sagebrush under an attempt to irrigate in order to hold reservoir rights granted under the Act of 1891... As most of the area irrigated prior to diversion by the Cain Irrigation Company was in old ranches it is probably that there was little change in the use from 1880 to 1920.[168]

The Mono Lake settlers practiced a mixed agricultural economy. Each homestead was both farm and ranch, raising crops and as many animals as possible. Most of the cultivated land was devoted to raising hay, which supplied winter feed for the cattle and sheep the settlers depended upon. A good harvest was almost certain every year, and the sizeable surplus fetched a good price—up to $50 per ton—in Bodie, Lundy and more distant places. It provided the major share of the farmers' income.[169]

After hay the most important crops were wheat and barley, relatively fast-growing grains; alfalfa, another forage crop which yielded two harvests each summer; and potatoes, which were ideally suited to the climatic and soil conditions in the basin.

Some of the farmers at Mono Lake specialized in raising potatoes... Each farmer tried to outdo the others in raising the largest potatoes... The harvesting...was quite a task. One man drove a horse hitched to a hand plough, which went up and down the rows of potatoes, turning over the soil and bringing the potatoes to the surface. The children of the families picked the potatoes up, sorting them as they went, and putting them into sacks. The smaller ones were hauled to dirt cellars and emptied into bins for winter use. The larger ones were sold in Lundy or Bodie.[17-]

Each farmhouse had a garden that produced a variety of vegetables, among them peas, beans, carrots, onions, strawberries and squash. The *Homer Mining Index* on June 28, 1883 looked forward to the ripening of "Mono Lake watermelons." Because of the short growing season, fruits were hard to grow, although pears were successfully raised in the 1890s at the Filosena farm between Mill and DeChambeau creeks[171], and, in a number of spots, old apple orchards still persist.

The ranchers also raised a large variety of animals. Pigs, goats, rabbits and chickens were confined near the farmhouses, while cattle, sheep, and horses roamed the countryside, often at considerable distances. The settlers depended on their stock for meat, milk, butter, cheese, eggs, wool and leather, and sold or traded surpluses at Bodie and Lundy.

The cattle, sheep and horses grazed the meadows and sagebrush scrub areas to the limits of their ever-decreasing carrying capacity. By the early 1880s, Mono Basin had already been grazed continuously for over 20 years. During the quiet period prior to the Bodie boom, settlers had practiced the same mixed agricultural and stock-raising economy, only on a smaller scale.

Settlers, however, had not been the only source of grazing pressure. In the 1860s, herdsmen had driven huge numbers of cattle and sheep through the Mono Basin via Bloody Canyon or Owens Valley en route to the fertile valleys of western Nevada, such as the Smith, Mason and Antelope valleys.[172] John Muir described the effects of this traffic on the vegetation at the head of Bloody Canyon:

> The vegetation of [Mono] pass has been in great part destroyed, and the same may be said of all the more accessible passes throughout the range. Immense numbers of starving sheep and cattle have been driven through them into Nevada, trampling the wild gardens and meadows out of existence.[173]

Geologist Israel Russell, who made his first visit to Mono Lake in 1881, also noted the effects of over-grazing:

> There was formerly sufficient wild grass in many portions of the basin to support considerable numbers of cattle and sheep; but, owing to overstocking, these natural pastures are now nearly ruined.[174]

Under pristine conditions, the sagebrush community which covers the lower slopes of the basin contained numerous perennial grasses, especially giant wildrye and Indian ricegrass. These grasses were not adapted to heavy grazing; the large native herbivores of the Great Basin, such as mule deer and pronghorn antelope, exerted little grazing pressure, preferring to browse on shrubs and forbs. The bunchgrasses were consumed by smaller species—sage grouse, rodents and insects—and the grass-seeds were harvested by the Kuzedika Paiute, but the effect was minimal. The Kuzedika probably enhanced the abundance of native bunchgrasses through their annual rabbit-drives, in which they lit fires in the sagebrush to force the rabbits into long net traps. The fires killed the sagebrush, but the bunchgrasses quickly resprouted from their roots, benefitting both from additional space and from the fertilizing nutrients freed from the tissues of the sagebrush.[175]

Cattle and sheep greatly reduced the perennial grasses and allowed the area covered by sagebrush to increase. As a result the capacity of the land to support stock steadily declined. Horses depleted the range as well; by the 1880s bands of feral horses roamed the Bodie Hills north of Mono Lake and the upper reaches of Sierran canyons.[176] In winter, while cattle and sheep were foddered on the ranches, the horse herds continued to graze on the native grasses.[177]

As the herds of cattle and sheep increased and the carrying capacity of the range declined, the ranchers were forced to find more distant pastures. It became standard practice to drive the animals into the Sierra Nevada during the summertime; the Curries, for example, drove their cattle from their ranch on the north shore of Mono Lake to summer range on the headwaters of the middle fork of the San Joaquin River southwest of June Lake.[178] As their herd grew, it became necessary to find winter pasture as well. They moved their animals about 70 miles south into the Owens Valley—a week-long drive in late fall and a return drive in spring.[179]

By the turn of the century, Basque, Spanish, Portuguese and French shepherds were driving large migratory bands of sheep, mostly from Kern County, along the eastern flank of the Sierra Nevada into Mono Basin. The sheep exerted considerable additional pressure on its grazing resources.[180] Entering Mono Basin in late spring, they grazed the sagebrush, meadows and cut-over pine forests until the passes and pastures in the Sierra were free of snow. In early summer the sheep were driven into the mountains, and at the end of the summer back the way they had come or down the western slope.[181]

The numbers of sheep were enormous. In 1903, 130,000 entered Mono Basin from the south;[182] the yearly influx was often closer to 200,000.[183] Although local residents benefitted to some extent from this influx—Mono County levied a license fee of five cents per head, the county's single largest source of revenues—competition for pasture became intense and led to increasingly hard feelings. Langille observed the situation in 1904:

Most of [the Basque and French shepherds who drove the sheep], as soon as they have accumulated a few hundred or thousand dollars return to their native land. Their business integrity is not questioned by any one and they are considered law-abiding in all respects except in the acquisition of range for their sheep. In this matter they do not regard either individual or Government rights, only so far as the actual fear of the law compels them to... Much friction exists between [migratory] sheep and [resident] cattle men. The cattlemen being land owners and tax payers feel that they should have rights to range, which are usurped by the nomadic sheepmen who invade their territory each season. The local sheep men also complain of range depredations by outsiders and being local tax payers consider themselves entitled to range from which they are driven... The whole region [including the southern half of Mono Basin] gave evidence of being greatly overstocked. There was absolutely nothing at all for horses to eat so thoroughly had the sheep gone over every part except the inclosures, and these had been stocked to depletion.[184]

In 1905 the migratory sheep were finally placed under stricter controls when much of the southern half of Mono Basin, from Lee Vining Creek south, was added to the Sierra Forest Reserve (which shortly became the Sierra National Forest). The reserve regulated grazing within its boundaries and gave priority to residents over transient stock-herders. Additional portions of the basin north of Lee Vining Creek and west of Mono Lake were protected in 1908 with the creation of the Mono National Forest, which subsumed those basin lands which had briefly been in the Sierra National Forest. National Forest policies continued to favor local stock-raisers, reducing the tensions over grazing access.

Migratory bands of sheep continued to graze in parts of the basin, but were no longer the "hoofed locusts" of former years. The flocks still had access to the sagebrush areas north, south and east of Mono Lake that were not in private hands. These "free lands," administered (or neglected) by the General Land Office, were not placed under grazing controls until passage of the Taylor Grazing Act of 1934. This act created the Bureau of Land Management, and withdrew these lands from private entry.[185] At present, grazing permits are required on all federally administered lands, and the sizes of herds are regulated.

Burcham estimated the magnitude of range depletion in the Great Basin:

the change in the acreage required to support an animal unit [the equivalent of one cow or steer, one horse or five sheep] has been greatest in the sagebrush plant community, which now requires about 2.6 times as much area as did the pristine range.[186]

Overgrazing also reduced the grazing capacity of meadows, where stripping of vegetation led to erosion and channel-cutting, which led in turn to desiccation of soils and further declines in grass abundance.[187]

Not only was the overall carrying capacity of the range drastically reduced, but its species composition was altered as well. By the turn of the century, alien weeds had invaded the overgrazed plant communities. Under heavy grazing conditions, these alien annuals had a decided advantage over native herbs and perennial grasses due primarily to reproductive characteristics derived from their evolution in heavily-grazed areas in southwest and central Asia. As the domestic animals from the Old World spread into the Great Basin, so too did the alien weeds.[188]

Post-boom

As the mines of the Bodie, Homer, Tioga and Jordan districts faltered and failed, the economy of Mono Basin became depressed. From 1878 to 1884, mining capital had fueled a period of local prosperity. But when the mines failed, shop owners, lumber companies, hotels, teamsters and stage lines failed as well; even the farmers and ranchers had to retrench. Henry DeGroot visited Bodie and Mono Basin in 1889, and described the state of affairs:

> With mining so depressed all other interests and branches of business have suffered in like degree. The town of Bodie and its surroundings show everywhere signs of decay. The former population of the place, amounting once to several thousand, has shrunk to a few hundred; more than half its stores and dwellings are empty. The big mills are all idle. A number of mills and hoisting works, once standing in the vicinity, have been torn down and removed elsewhere, some of those left being partially dismantled or dilapidated beyond repair. The railroad extending to Mono Lake, built during the bonanza era...has been stripped of its rolling stock and gone to decay. The sawmills in the Sierra have shut down and the woodchopper's occupation is gone, while the stock raisers and farmers, left without an available market for their products, are generally poor, nor can any of these interests or classes hope for a greater prosperity until the business of mining itself shall have become more prosperous.[189]

After 1890, mining at Bodie was largely restricted to the reduction of low-grade ores and old tailings; new methods made these previously worthless sources profitable. In 1892 the world's first long-distance power line brought electricity to the Standard Mine at Bodie from water-driven turbines on Green Creek in Bridgeport Basin 12 miles away. Although a costly ($38,000) and experimental project, it replaced the 200 cords of wood consumed each month to fuel the Standard stamp-mill, and saved the company about $25,000 per year, quickly paying for itself.[190]

Mining also continued in Homer and Jordan districts, but, compared to former years, in a subdued way. In 1894 the *Homer Mining Index* was again struggling and hoping in the now quiet village of Lundy. Advertisements give an idea of what Lundy was like: two hotels, Hotel Monte at the head and Lake House at the foot of Lundy Lake; the Montrose Lumber yard, offering lumber at $35 per thousand board feet, or $40 delivered; three general stores, a grocery, a blacksmith's shop and a bakery. One surveyor, one doctor, one undertaker and two lawyers were sufficient to meet the needs of the town and the surrounding area. The *Index* still saw the mines as the source of future prosperity:

> If there were ready sales of the produce that could be raised, nearly all the land around [Mono] Lake would be valuable. There is room for quite a colony. All hands are looking forward to the time when Jordan shall start up and enliven things.[191]

The editor was anticipating the re-opening of the Detroit Copper Mine; the event occurred with some fanfare:

> The boom was caused by a stock promotion deal and there was quite a sum of money spent. A large mill was built and a ditch three miles long was dug to bring water from Mill Creek to operate the mill. The excitement brought many new people into the area and soon there was a little town at the foot of Copper Mountain, which took for its name 'Copper Mountain.' Two merchandise stores were built; ...there were two saloons, a large blacksmith shop and a post office. When the post office was established, the name of the town was changed to Jordan.[192]

But, by 1900, the mine was closed again, and Jordan practically abandoned. Intermittent work in the mine continued until 1908, when it closed for good.[193]

The Annual Reports of the State Mineralogist from 1892 to 1896 list 13 working mines in Homer District, most of them small ones on Mt. Scowden. The May Lundy had been re-opened in 1889 after five idle years, and together with the adjacent Jackson and Lakeview mines (all three now under the ownership of the Jackson and Lakeview Company), was delivering ore via a 2,560-foot-long tramway to a new ten-stamp mill in Lake Canyon. The mill was water-powered, driven by the waters of Lake Oneida through a pipe 760 feet long. In 1896 the Jackson and Lakeview Company employed 47 men. As before, the May Lundy veins proved to be profitable, although no longer rich. In 1900 the property was purchased by the Crystal Lake Gold Mining Company, and the stamp-mill was increased to 20 stamps.[194] The mine was worked for another 15 years. Total production between 1889 and 1915 was slightly over $1 million,[195] for an average annual yield of about $40,000, far below the output of the earlier period.

The continued success of the May Lundy was the exception. As mining activity dwindled, ranching and farming became the mainstays of the economy. Little incentive existed for surplus production, however, because there was little market locally and transportation to outside areas was poor and costly. The basin was never linked by rail to the outside world, although plans and even surveys were made as late as 1910.[196] At the turn of the century, the people of Mono Basin lived their lives in relative isolation, with the prospect of a quiet future.

POSTSCRIPT

Lt. Tredwell Moore's expedition of 1852—with its brutal treatment of Indians and discovery of gold—set the tone for the white occupation of Mono Basin. That occupation, initially motivated by the desire for instant wealth, proved to be disastrous for the native Indians. When the setters and miners forced the Kuzedika off their lands, an alien economy replaced a stable and ecologically viable mode of life, one perfectly adapted to the Mono Basin environment. The white economy was based on intensive exploitation, most obviously of minerals and lumber, but also of rangelands. It was unstable, with bust following boom. It even exploited the Kuzedika themselves for cheap labor on ranches, in sawmills and along the railroad.

To the basin's farmers and ranchers at the turn of the century, their way of life seemed stable enough. Like the Kuzedika, they had become self-sufficient and independent, and had no inkling that they too would be dispossessed by a stronger, distant society. But life in the basin was to change again, radically.

The early years of the twentieth century saw the beginning of a series of contests over the right to exploit the one still-bountiful resource of Mono Basin—its water. As early as 1904 plans were afoot that would eventually bring the farming and ranching era to a close. In that year an engineer, Thomas Means, visited Mono Basin with two companions, Fred Eaton, former mayor of Los Angeles, and J. B. Lippincott, chief of Reclamation Service operations in the Southwest. According to Means' summary of the trip,

Mr. Eaton's plan of supplying Los Angeles from the Owens River was discussed and in the visit to Mono Basin the possibility of diverting the waters of Rush Creek by means of a tunnel to Long Valley on Owens River was mentioned.[1]

Although it would take time to bring these plans to fruition, the days of the Mono Basin farmers were numbered.

Over the next 30 years ranchers, farmers, local irrigation and electric power companies and the city of Los Angeles waged a complicated battle to hold onto or obtain water rights. The victor was the city, which by the mid-1930s had purchased land or water rights along the five principal tributaries of Mono Lake—Walker, Parker, Rush, Lee Vining and Mill creeks—and littoral rights along Mono Lake's shore, at a total cost of approximately $5 million. The money offered by the city to the strapped landowners struggling through the Great Depression was too tempting. In many cases they were allowed to live for a time where they always had. When Los Angeles began to divert water from the basin in 1940, however, the residents who objected had insufficient legal power to do so successfully.[2] For all practical purposes, the city had displaced them from their lands as surely as the settlers had earlier displaced the Kuzedika.

The results of Los Angeles' water diversions from Mono Basin streams have been many: the loss of irrigation water, and hence drastic declines in farming and ranching; the steadily dropping levels of Mono Lake, with associated increases in salinity and alkalinity; the lowering of the groundwater table, with impacts on riparian and shoreline vegetation; the desiccation of the lower reaches of streams, with loss of fisheries and river habitat; and, notably, increasing awareness of the beauties and frailties of Mono Basin's landscape. I hope that the history of resource exploitation, whose early stages I have charted here, does not culminate in the sacrifice of the great natural values which still remain—and that J. Ross Browne's description of Mono Lake as the "Dead Sea of the West" never becomes an accurate one.

APPENDICES

APPENDIX I: Letters from Lt. Tredwell Moore to the Pacific Division

The originals of these letters are at the National Archives, Washington D.C.

Letter 1

Hd Qrs Fort Miller, Cal.
June 12th, 1852

Sirs

Information was received at this post a few days since, that the Indians on the head waters of the Merced had made an attack on eight white men who were "prospecting" the south fork of that river. Three of the whites were killed, and two were severely wounded. A party of miners, after the news came in, went in pursuit of the Indians. They did not succeed in overtaking them but have I believe recovered the bodies of the killed. The Indians who committed the murders belong to the Yo-sem-i-ties, of whom complaint was made to the Genl. Comds. last winter. They have committed many robberies, but have until this last act, refrained from murder. I will start in pursuit of them on Monday next, and endeavor not only to punish the Indians who were engaged in committing the murder, but also to remove the tribe to the reservation set aside for them by the commissioners last year. Qr. Masters funds will be necessary to carry on the Expedition. Enclosed you will find requisitions for funds and stores, which please submit to the General Comds. as early as convenient.

Capt. E. D. Townsend
Ass. Adj. Genl.
Benicia, Cal.

I am sir very
respect-
fully
Your obt Srvt
T Moore

Letter 2

Head Quarters Camp Steele
Near the Head Waters of the Merced
July 8th, 1852

Sir

I have the honor to report that, I arrived at my present encampment on the Head Waters of the Merced on the 20th of June, immediately on my arrival scouting parties were sent to scour the country in all directions. Many deserted "Rancherias" were found, but no Indians. The friendly Indians we had with us as guides are of the opinion that the entire tribe had crossed the Sierras. Major Savage with a party of Indians struck a fresh trail heading from the valley towards the head waters of the San Joaquin, his provisions giving out he was obliged to return. On the 1st I took with me a party of twelve men and taking Major Savage's trail soon came to a heavy trail. This we continued to follow. And on the morning of the 4th crossed the main ridge of the Sierra. I encamped about noon and sending out scouts I received information that there was a "Rancheria" some four miles distant, by dividing my party I was enabled to take them so completely by surprise that before they were able to move they were entirely surrounded. Twenty-one prisoners were taken—six men, the remainder women and children—one of the prisoners acknowledged that they saw the murders of the whites on the Merced, but denied having participated in it. A number of trinkets together with some clothing was found which fully implicated their participation in the division of the murdered men's property, if not in the murder. The men I then ordered to be shot which was done on the morning of the 5th. From the women taken I have learned that it was a general thing and that nearly the entire tribe was present at the murder. Lieut. McLean started for Yo Semity Valley on the 1st with ten men with instructions to destroy the "Rancherias" and provisions there, he succeeded in finding a large quantity of acorns which were destroyed. One of his men (Riley) was severely wounded receiving two arrow shots on the night of the 4th while on post as sentinel. Lieut. McLean arrived this morning, having accomplished the destruction of as much property and provisions as could be found. Riley the wounded man died last night. Mr. Crosby will hand you requisition which please submit to the Genl. Commanding at your earliest opportunity.

Capt. E. D. Townsend
Ass. Adjt. Genl.
Pacific Division
San Francisco, Cala.

I am Sir
Very Respectfully
Your obdt Servt.
T. Moore
1st Lt. Infantry
Comdg. Expedition

Letter 3

Hd. Qrs. Camp Steele
July 9th, 1852

Sir

From information received from the Indian women taken a few days since, I have determined to follow the Yosemities across the Sierras, into the Mono country. The Yo semitis are on friendly terms with the Monos and have fled to this country thinking that the whites will not follow them across the snow. A few families are yet scattered in the vallies high up in the mountains, but are making their way as rapidly as possible to the Mono territory. The squad taken on the 4th was one of these detached parties. The Indians inform me that mules can be taken across the mountains without much difficulty— In connection with this I would state that my command is so small, that I cannot with prudence detach men from it to guard the pack train. This up to the present, has not been necessary, but my farther movement in the mountains will require that the train have a small escort for the safe transmission of supplies. I would respectfully suggest that a small detachment of dragoons be sent to me for that purpose—I would also state that the necessity of detaching two and three men as scouts, without other arms than muskets, has led me to think that a few six shooters would be of service for parties of this nature. Enclosed I transmit a requisition for ten which I hope will meet the approbation of the Genl Comdg.

Capt. E. D. Townsend
Ass. Adj. Genl.
Pacific Division
San Francisco, Cal.

I am Sir very
respectfully
Your
obt servt.
T. Moore
Lt. In'try

APPENDIX II: Newspaper Accounts

ITEM 1: Report describing Lt. Moore's expedition into Mono Basin as published in *Stockton Journal*, August 24, 1852; an identical report, copied from the *Stockton Journal*, appeared in *Alta California*, San Francisco, on August 26, 1852.

NEWS FROM THE MOUNTAINS—GOLD DISCOVERIES BEYOND THE SIERRA—

From Mr. Crosby, quarter master U.S.A., in Mariposa, we learn the particulars of a recent expedition beyond the mountains, under command of Lieut. Moore. The expedition was composed of dragoons, and left the Fresno about twenty days since, in search of Indians. They pursued an easterly direction to the head of the Middle Fork of the Merced River, when they struck through a trail that led across the mountains, heretofore deemed impassible, which they followed until safely arrived on the opposite side of the first range of the Sierra Nevada. Here they entered upon a region resembling the San Joaquin Valley near the mountains, except that it displayed a more barren appearance, and seemed more deserted than the hills on this side. After descending into the plains and marching a short distance in search of Indians, they discovered, about fifteen miles from the base of the hills, a large lake some twenty-five or thirty miles long, by the same measurement in width, which they named Lake Mono, after the tribe of Indians that inhabit that section. This lake does not appear to have any outlet, and is of a very brackish taste. There are several streams of pure water—two of considerable magnitude—emptying into it, on the borders of which is the only wood to be found. Sea gulls, geese, and ducks abound on its waters, and its banks are covered with *tache le mere* and sand.

There is very little good land to attract the settler. The country around is cut up with trails, and it is supposed there are more Indians east than west of the mountains. Cattle, horse, and mule tracks are abundant. The Mono Indians manifested considerable surprise at the appearance of the dragoons in their country, but appeared to be friendly. Several were taken prisoners, treated with kindness and turned loose. The California Indians made several attacks on the Americans, killing three or four horses, but doing no other mischief.

Mr. Crosby reports the finding of gold on the other side of the mountains, both in placers and quartz. Several specimens have been brought back, which were collected from the placers on the eastern slope, which would induce the belief that the diggings were of coarse gold. Water is scarce, but mostly in springs, which run only a few miles, and lose themselves in the sand. The Tuolumne and San Joaquin head up near the large lake, showing there are several passages through the mountains.

Yosemitz, an influential chief of the California Indians, has gone over among the Monos, since the death of Major Savage, and it is thought he will influence the tribe on that side against the whites.

We have not space this morning to give an extended notice of this expedition, but will try and do it at some future time, when we become more fully possessed of the facts.

ITEM 2: Note on Moore's request for reinforcements from *Alta California*, San Francisco, July 15, 1852.

"More Indian Difficulties"—Capt. [sic] Crosby, Quartermaster's Agent, arrived in this city [Stockton] last evening, on his way to Benicia for reinforcements, to join Lieut. Moore on the headwaters of the Merced. He informs us that on the evening of the 4th inst. Lieut. Moore came up with the Indians who killed the two miners recently, and routed the rancheria, killing six and taking twelve prisoners. Lt. Moore lost one man. Farther difficulty is expected with these Indians, and Lieut. Moore will await the arrival of reinforcements on the middle fork of the Merced, where he is encamped.

ITEM 3: Report describing von Schmidt's baseline extension from the *Sacramento Daily Union*, August 8, 1855

Survey over the Sierra Nevada

It gives us pleasure to announce the safe return of Capt. A. W. Von Schmidt, United States Deputy Surveyor, to this city, on Thursday last. With a party of twelve men and eighteen mules; the Captain was detailed by Col. Hays, United States Surveyor General, to survey and establish permanently the Mount Diablo base line across the Sierra Nevada mountains, to or near the State line. We are indebted to Capt. Von Schmidt for many facts and incidents connected with his tour, which are of a highly interesting character.

The company left Stockton on the 4th of June, and, pursuing their course in this direction, extended the line east, from a point near the foot hills, formerly run by Col. Norris, and passing thence about two miles north of Chinese Camp, and six miles south of Sonora—placing this city in range sixteen east of Mount Diablo. The line crosses the Tuolumne River above Ward's Ferry. Owing to the zigzag course of the stream, he was compelled to cross the South Fork of the Tuolumne three times, the country being very rough and mountainous. No settlements were seen east of the South Fork. He represents the country, however, as abounding in timber of the finest qualities—pine, spruce, hemlock, etc. The valleys are narrow and the soil poor. Leaving the Tuolumne drainage, he came to the head-waters of the Merced, the sources of which he found high up in the highest mountains, covered with beds of snow, and cut up by deep ravines, the crossing of which, with mules, was very hazardous. The timber in this region was not so good. He next came to the sources of the San Joaquin, which he found extended within ten miles of the valley on the other side of the mountains, and at such an altitude that the timber attains but a very diminutive growth, the summits being covered with snow about nine months of the year.

On one of these elevations, where ravines descended from three to four thousand feet in depth, and in about range twenty-five east of Mount Diablo, the Captain experienced great difficulty in keeping his party and train together; so, deputing his assistant, Mr. Clement Cox, with six men, in charge of the line, he undertook to conduct the train to the valley on the other side of the mountains. Encountering an impassable ravine, and failing to meet Mr. Cox at a designated point, he traveled all day, and finally encamped near a large lake, formed by some of the branches of the San Joaquin. The next day, ascending some of the highest peaks, several hours were spent in building fires, in hopes to arrest the attention of the missing party, who finally came up, with one exception, having been thirty hours without food or rest. After a day's rest, the missing man, Mr. Lynch, not making his appearance, the party proceeded with their work, leaving in camp provisions and directions, should he return. It was several days afterward, however, when he made his appearance, much fatigued, having sustained life by killing a ground-hog with the ram-rod of his gun, his ammunition being exhausted.

A few days after this, seven men were again dispatched with the line, and succeeded in crossing into the valley, on the other side of the Sierra Nevadas, Capt. Von Schmidt bringing up the train. Toiling over sharp-broken, precipitous rocks, where the trail could be traced by the blood on the animals' feet, which were literally cut to pieces, at the end of the third day he found all but two of the party in the same ravine where he had previously descended. Having undergone much fatigue, and having been without food for three days, they were so weak as scarcely to be able to walk, and the joy of the Captain on seeing and being able to relieve their condition, can be better imagined than described.

The two who were absent, Redman and Lynch, had been sent in search of the train, and did not return to the main party till two days afterwards, being five days without food. Their voices were low and their steps laggard; but after three days' rest, they were again ready to resume duty.

All again together, the party proceeded with their work, locating the line about two miles south of Lake Mono, a beautiful sheet of salt water, some fifteen miles in diameter, and around which are to be seen numerous old volcanic mountains, their craters still visible. Capt. Von Schmidt represents the entire surface of the country in this region as composed of pumice-stone, but the scenery often beautiful in the extreme, all the head waters of the streams abounding in lakes or basins, near the summit of the mountains. The base line was run as far as what is supposed to be the State line, in ranges thirty and thirty-one, east of Mount Diablo. Six miles east of this stretches a high ridge of mountains, between which and the Sierra Nevadas lies the valley through which flows Owen's river towards the desert. In this valley he encountered numerous Indians of the Mono tribe, a rather superior race, who at times manifested great uneasiness, being unable to comprehend the object of the surveying party, but who were appeased by trifling presents. Extending the standard line south of the base for seventy-two miles, and encountering no land of any value, it was resolved to return—an announcement which was received by the weary party with decided approbation.

It was the original design of the Captain to return by Walker's river pass; but at Lake Mono he was informed by a young Indian chief who spoke Spanish, of the existence of a trail by which he could reach Sonora in five days. He took this trail, which is described as almost impassable. Notwithstanding the precipitousness of the mountains, however, on the fourteenth day with his party he reached Duncan's valley—fourteen miles east of this city. The last ten days of the tour was accomplished under circumstances more painful than any other, if possible. The provisions of the party being exhausted, they were compelled to subsist on a small daily allowance of flour, what berries they could fine, and catnip tea—traveling from fifteen to twenty miles a day.

Capt. Von Schmidt is a Russian by birth, and is a man of fine intelligence and extraordinary energy. He has accomplished all he undertook to do, and returned in fine health and spirits, after encountering extreme hardship and privation. His description of the country and his adventures possess much interest, and we regret having to condense them within so limited a space. He accomplished the journey without losing a man, and but three mules. He proceeds at once to San Francisco, to report to Col. Hays, the United States Surveyor General.

NOTES

Chapter 1: THE BACKGROUND

The Physical Setting

1. Loeffler, 1977, 15.

2. Reveal, 1965, 104.

3. Munz and Keck, 1968, 10-11.

4. Vasek and Thorne, 1977, 810.

5. Rundel et al., 1977, 577.

The Kuzedika Paiute

6. Steward, 1933, 236.

7. E. Davis, 1964, 257-259; Bettinger, 1982, 58.

8. E. Davis, 1965, 36. The Kuzedika's near-neighbors and relations, the Owens Valley Paiute, practiced irrigation to augment their food supply (Steward, 1933, 247-250; Lawton et. al., 1976), but the Kuzedika never attempted any sort of agriculture (Bettinger, 1982, 24) .

9. Steward, 1933, 257-58.

10. E. Davis, 1965, 25-26.

11. Steward, 1933, 243-245; Davis, 1965, 33.

12. The collection of *kutsavi* by the Kuzedika and other Great Basin Indians has been the subject of a large literature. See Heizer (1950) for a bibliography.

13. E. Davis, 1962, 27.

14. Aldrich, 1921, 36-38; Steward, 1933, 256; E. Davis, 1965, 29-32.

15. Muir, 1911, 206; Steward, 1933, 255.

16. Muir, 1911, 227.

17. D. Davis, 1964, map 2.

18. Steward, 1933, 257; J. Davis, 1961, 20-21).

19. J. Davis, 1961, 21-22.

20. Steward, 1933, 257-58.

21. Steward, 1933, 329.

Chapter 2: EARLIEST EXPLORATIONS, 1827-1857

Legendary Discoverers: Jedediah Smith and Joseph Walker

1. Farquhar, 1965, 27-28.

2. Bancroft, 1885, v. III, 152-157.

3. Sprague's letter, to Edmund Randolph, was first published in Randolph's *Address on the History of California*, San Francisco, Sept. 10, 1860; subsequently it appeared in the San Francisco *Bulletin* and other coast papers in Oct. 1860, and in *Hutching's Magazine*, Feb. 1861. See Farquhar (1965, 28) for a note on Sprague's factual errors.

4. Angel, 1881, 21.

5. Angel, 1881, p. 21; also known as Thompson and West's *History of Nevada*, recently reprinted by Howell-North Books, Berkeley, California. Letter is quoted in Chalfant (1922, 94-95), where it is accepted at face value; and in Chappell (1947, 246). I have used Chappell's quotation with her bracketed comments.

6. Farquhar, 1965, 25.

7. Farquhar, 1965, 26.

8. Ewers, 1959, 65.

9. Robert Heizer, an authority on California and Great Basin Indians, concludes from this passage that Mono Lake must have been the site of Leonard's observations (1950, 35-41).

10. Ewers, 1959, 73.

11. Stewart, 1941, 373, 426-27; in addition, entomologist David Herbst has recently collected pupae of brine flies "from numerous ephemeral ponds in the Carson Sink" (personal communication, 1981).

12. Loew, 1876; Steward, 1933; Aldrich, 1921.

13. Ewers, 73-74.

14. Russell, 1885, 225.

15. Scott Stine, personal communication, 1986.

16. Ewers, 1959, 74.

17. Farquhar, 1965, 36.

18. Watson, 1934, 105.

The Discovery of Mono Basin: Lt. Tredwell Moore's Expedition of 1852

19. In keeping with a tradition in the Regular Army, Lt. Moore probably named Camp Steele in honor of his fellow officer Frederick Steele, Adjutant, Second Infantry, stationed at the time in Monterey (personal communication with George Stammerjohan, Historian, California Department of Parks and Recreation, Sacramento).

20. Russell, 1951, 54.

21. In the search for Lt. Moore's summary report of his 1852 Mono Basin expedition, the following files of U.S. Army and Bureau of Indian Affairs correspondence have been examined:

i. Registers of Letters Received by the Pacific Division for 1852 and 1853; checked under the names of Moore and his subordinates Lts. McLean and Crosby. The three letters reproduced here came from these files at the National Archives, Washington D.C.

ii. Records of the Second Infantry (Record Group 391, Records of U.S. Regular Army Mobile Units, 1821-1942). No correspondence files for 1852. National Archives.

iii. Registers of Letters Received by the Adjutant General's Office (from either Lt. Moore or Ethan A. Hitchcock, Commander of the Pacific Division). National Archives.

iv. Registers of Letters Received by the Commanding General of the Army (RG 108, Records of the Headquarters of the Army). National Archives.

v.Registers of Letters Received by the Secretary of War (RG 107, Records of the Office of the Secretary of War). National Archives.

vi.Registers of Letters Received by the Bureau of Indian Affairs Pertaining to the War Department, June 1852-June 30, 1853. National Archives.

vii.Registers of Letters Received by the Bureau of Indian Affairs Pertaining to the California [Indian] Superintendency (M234, rolls 32-52). Federal Archives and Records Center, San Bruno, California.

22. Bunnell, 277.

23. Bunnell, 278.

24. Bunnell, 278.

25. As shown on Eddy's map, Lt. Moore named Mono Lake, and gave various tributary streams names honoring his men: McLeans R., Crosbys R., Fraser Cr., Watts Cr., Cranes Cr. He named the two islands Beauty (Negit) and Grand (Paoha). The map is in the possession of the Bancroft Library, University of California, Berkeley. See Wheat (1942, 117-118) for a discussion of Eddy's map (No. 257 in Wheat's book, which does not reproduce it).

The First Suveys: A. W. von Schmidt

26. Ernst, 1949, 27. Ernst describes von Schmidt's route through Yosemite National Park. Ernst knew nothing of Lt. Moore's expedition, and thought von Schmidt was the first white man through this area.

27. von Schmidt, 1855, 53-54.

28. Chalfant, 1922, Chapter 9.

29. Lawton et al., 1976, 21-27.

30. Stine, 1981.

31. See Ernst (1949) for a general appraisal of von Schmidt's accuracy. For a detailed demonstration of the quality of his work, see Stine (1981).

Chapter 3: EARLY SETTLEMENT, 1852-1877

Dogtown, Monoville and Aurora

1. Bunnell, 1881, 278; Maule, 1938, 5.

2. Russell, 1947, 118.

3. Hoover, 1966, 212.

4. Kersten, 1964, 495.

5. Maule, 1938, 8.

6. Russell, 1947, 118.

7. Chalfant, 1922, 127.

8. Kersten, 1964, 495.

9. DeGroot, 1890, 343.

10. Kersten, 1964 495; Calhoun, 1967, 73.

11. The remains of Dogtown, visible at the turnoff to Bodie from U.S. 395, have been designated State Registered Landmark 792. "Dogtown" was a popular name among miners for a camp built of huts or hovels "good enough for dogs to live in" (Gudde, 1965, 87).

12. Chalfant 1922, 126; Wedertz, 1978, 25.

13. Colcord, 1928, 113.

14. DeGroot was for many years a leading expert on California and Nevada mines and mining, and at various times was employed by the state to report on mining conditions and developments. See Wheat (1957, v. 5, pt. 1, 13-18 and 66-68) for discussions of DeGroot's contributions to the early cartography of the mining regions and for a short biographical sketch.

15. DeGroot, 1860, 8.

16. Colcord, 1928, 113.

17. DeGroot, 1860, 8; Paul, 1947, 120.

18. Maule, 1938, 45.

19. *Bancroft Scraps*, v. 2, 692.

20. DeGroot, 1860, 8.

21. The estimate of 900 is given in what appears to be a contemporary newspaper clipping contained in *Bancroft Scraps*, v. 2, p. 694, where it is dated 1861. The clipping, however, is from Browne (1868, 178), not from a newspaper, and is misdated. Browne bases his estimate upon a census taken at Monoville in 1860. The estimate of 3,000 appears in Chalfant (1922, 127), with no authority given; it is almost certainly much too high.

22. Browne, 1869, 400-402. Browne, like DeGroot, was a highly respected observer of California and Nevada mining. While on a variety of official commissions for the federal government (e.g., Browne, 1868), Browne wrote popular and informative accounts of his travels, many of which were published in *Harper's Magazine* before coming out in book form. His *A Peep at Washoe* and *Washoe Revisited*, describing life in the Comstock, became his most popular writings on the West. The passages quoted here were originally published in *Harper's* in 1865, in "A Trip to Bodie Bluff and the Dead Sea of the West," and were reprinted in 1869 at the end of *Adventures in Apache Country*, which described a trip through Arizona. For a discussion of his career as a secret federal agent, see Dillon (1965).

23. Kersten, 1964, 495.

24. Homer Mining Index, July 17, 1880.

25. Whiting, 1888, 366.

26. Aurora was so close to the (as yet unsurveyed) boundary between the State of California and Nevada Territory that during the years 1861 to 1863 the town served as the seat of two counties simultaneously. For discussions of this political anomaly see Chappell (1947) and Thomas (1952).

27. Kersten, 1964, 497; Colcord, 1928, 119.

28. Brewer, 1930, 409.

29. Brewer, 1930, 415-416.

30. Muir, 1916, 96.

31. Chappell, 1947, 244; Buckbee, 1935, 376-377.

32. Maule, 1938, 30, 52, 56; Kersten, 1964, 499-500.

33. Browne, 1869, 396, 415, 443.

34. Brewer, 1930, 418.

35. For a discussion of the 1861 Clayton map, see Wheat (1957, v. 5, pt. 1, 19n) and Maule (1938, 12). A copy of the map is in the Bancroft Library, University of California, Berkeley.

36. Maule, 1938, 5; Farquhar, 1928, 83-84.

The Quiet Period, 1865-1877

37. Kersten, 1964, 502.

38. Chappell, 1947, 245.

39. DeGroot, 1890, 344.

40. LeConte, 1875, 118.

41. Browne, 1869, 430; LeConte 1875, 118.

42. Browne, 1869, 432-434.

43. LeConte, 1875, 118.

44. LeConte, 1875, 116.

45. E. Davis, 1965, 7.

46. LeConte, 1875, 114.

47. Muir, 1911, 206; LeConte, 1875, 105, 114; Calhoun, 1967, 32.

48. Muir, 1911, 206; Calhoun, 1967, 32.

49. Muir, 1911, 226.

50. Calhoun, 1967, 22, 31; E. Davis, 1965, 8.

51. Muir, 1916, 245-246.

CHAPTER 4: Boom and Bust, 1877-1900

Bodie

1. Wasson, 1878, 5-6.

2. Wasson, 1878, 6.

3. Wasson, 1878, 6.

4. Silliman, 1864, 13.

5. Silliman, 1864, 31.

6. Silliman, 1864, 35.

7. Silliman, 1864, 35-36.

8. Smith, 1925, 67.

9. Browne, 1869, 418-419.

10. Browne, 1869, 416-418.

11. Wasson, 1878, 7-8.

12. Cain, 1956, 15.

13. Smith, 1925, 68.

14. Wasson, 1878, 6.

15. Parr, 1928, 33.

16. Wasson, 1878, 27; Parr, 1928, 35.

17. Wedertz, 1969, 131.

18. Wasson, 1878, 20.

19. Wasson, 1878, 20; Johnson, 1967, 22.

20. *Bodie Weekly Standard(D), December 12, 1877.*

21. *Bodie Weekly Standard*, November 28, 1877.

22. *Bodie Weekly Standard*, December 12, 1877.

23. *Bodie Weekly Standard*, January 30, 1878.

24. *Bodie Weekly Standard*, February 6, 1878.

25. Wasson, 1878, 20-22.

26. Wasson, 1878, 22.

27. Smith, 1925, 68; Parr, 1928, 36-37.

28. *Mono Alpine Chronicle*, December 7, 1878.

29. *Mono Alpine Chronicle*, December 21, 1878.

30. Wasson, 1879, xv.

31. Smith, 1925, 68.

32. Smith, 1925, 69-70.

33. *Homer Mining Index*, July 7, 1880.

34. Estimates of a peak population of 10,000 and even 15,000 appear in popular histories of Bodie, but are unfounded. Bodie newspapers occasionally gave such high figures (e.g., *Daily Free Press*, November 6, 1879), but the great majority of newspaper estimates were much more conservative, agreeing with the reports of reliable authorities such as Wasson, Whiting and DeGroot on a peak population for 1879 and 1880 of about 5,000. Colcord (1928, 119n.) states that "there were never more than 5,000 people living in Bodie...at any one time." The census figure printed in the *Homer Mining Index* is the highest reliable estimate known.

35. Smith, 1925, 76; Whiting, 1888, 383.

36. Whiting, 1888, 383.

37. Whiting, 1888, 397; Clark, 1970, 13.

Bodie as a Stimulus to Development in Mono Basin

38. Browne, 1869, 416.

Mining in the Mono Basin

39. Shinn, 1885, 118.

40. Paul, 1947, 215.

41. Johnson, 1967, 27.

42. Maule, 1938, 17.

43. *Bodie Weekly Standard*, November 28, 1877.

44. *Mammoth City Herald*, July 18, 1880.

Lundy and Homer Districts

45. Browne, 1869, 443.

46. Maule, 1938, 44.

47. *Bodie Standard* and *Mammoth City Herald*, September, 1879; *Homer Mining Index*, June 12, 1880.

48. *Homer Mining Index*, June 12, 1880.

49. *Homer Mining Index*, June 12, 1880.

50. *Homer Mining Index*, September 24, 1879.

51. *Mammoth City Herald*, September 24, 1879.

52. *Homer Mining Index*, June 19, 1880.

53. McIntosh, 1908, 24; DeDecker, 1966, 19.

54. Whiting, 1888, 370-371.

55. Whiting, 1888, 369.

56. The town of Wasson has been mistakenly located by Maule (1938, overlay, Bridgeport Quadrangle) and DeDecker (1966, 18), where it is placed in Lake Canyon.

57. *Mammoth City Herald*, September 24, 1879.

58. *Mammoth City Herald*, September 24, 1879.

59. *Homer Mining Index*, June 12, 1880.

60. *Homer Mining Index*, June 19, 1880.

61. *Homer Mining Index* , June 12, 1880.

62. *Homer Mining Index*, June 26, 1880.

63. *Homer Mining Index*, August 20, 1881.

64. *Homer Mining Index*, October 1, 1881.

65. Whiting, 1888, 369.

66. *Homer Mining Index*, October 2, 1880.

67. *Homer Mining Index*, November 2, 1880.

68. *Homer Mining Index*, November 20, 1880.

69. *Homer Mining Index*, November 9, 1880.

70. Maule, 1938, 45; *Mammoth City Herald*, September 24, 1879.

71. *Homer Mining Index*, August 21, 1880.

72. *Homer Mining Index*, June 24, 1882.

73. McIntosh, 1908, 89.

74. Whiting, 1888, 369.

75. A hiatus exists in the run of extant issues of the *Homer Mining Index* from early August 1882 to mid-June 1883; detailed information for this period is therefore lacking.

76. *Homer Mining Index*, October 27, 1883.

77. *Homer Mining Index*, November 3, 1883.

78. *Homer Mining Index*, November 10, 1883.

79. *Homer Mining Index*, May 17, 1884.

80. *Homer Mining Index*, August 23, 1884.

81. Whiting, 1888, 369.

Bennettville and the Tioga District

82. *Homer Mining Index*, January 5, 1884; Hubbard, 1958, 2.

83. Russell, 1947, 119.

84. Russell, 1947, 119.

85. *Homer Mining Index*, October 10, 1881. Very little information exists regarding most of the claims in Tioga District, no doubt because none of them proved to be productive. The estimate of 350 claims appears in *Homer Mining Index*, October 1, 1881, where many of the mines are listed by name, located (vaguely), and described. No production figures for any of them exist.

86. *Homer Mining Index*, September 17, 1881.

87. *Homer Mining Index*, September 17, 1881.

88. *Homer Mining Index*, April 6, 1881.

89. Hubbard, 1958, unpaginated.

90. *Homer Mining Index*, February 18, 1882.

91. *Homer Mining Index*, March 4, 1882; Smith, 1929, 25-27. See Russell (1947, 119-120) for the text of the *Homer Mining Index* article describing this exploit.

92. Whiting, 1888, 371-373; Hubbard, 1958, unpaginated.

93. Trexler, 1961, 5.

94. *Homer Mining Index*, June 23, 1883.

95. Trexler, 1961, 4-7.

96. Hubbard, 1958, unpaginated.

97. Hubbard, 1958, unpaginated.

98. Whiting, 1888, 372.

99. Hubbard, 1958, unpaginated.

Jordan and Vernon Districts

100. Browne, 1868, 178.

101. *Homer Mining Index*, May 6, 1882.

102. *Homer Mining Index*, July 17, 1880.

103. *Homer Mining Index*, December 31, 1881.

104. *Homer Mining Index*, February 11, 1881.

105. *Homer Mining Index*, October 1, 1881.

106. *Homer Mining Index*, November 3, 1883.

107. Whiting, 1888, 366.

108. Whiting, 1888, 365.

109. *Homer Mining Index*, May 27, 1882.

110. *Homer Mining Index*, July 3, 1880.

111. *Homer Mining Index*, June 10, 1882.

112. *Homer Mining Index*, June 17, 1882.

Lumbering in Mono Basin

113. Smith, 1925, 68-69; *Bodie Standard Weekly*, November 14, 1877.

114. Wedertz, 1969, 156.

115. Billeb, 1957.

116. Wedertz, 1969, 156.

117. Muir, 1916, 244.

Mono Mills

118. *Weekly Standard News*, October 12, 1881.

119. Myrick (1962, 298-313) and Billeb (1968) provide excellent accounts of the construction and operations of the Bodie railroad. Wedertz (1969, 158-161) contains supplemental information.

120. Myrick, 1962, 307.

121. Langille, 1904b, 14. The spring is located in section 10, T1S, R28E.

122. Billeb, 1957.

123. *Bodie Weekly Standard News*, October 12, 1881; Billeb, 1968, 54-55.

124. Wedertz, 1969, 158.

125. *Homer Mining Index*, July 8, 1882.

126. Myrick, 1962, 309; Wedertz, 1969, 161.

127. Billeb, 1957.

128. Whiting, 1888, 383.

129. Myrick, 1962, 312.

130. Langille, 1904a, 33-36.

131. Langille, 1904a and 1904b.

132. Langille, 1904a, 34.

133. Billeb, 1968, 199.

134. Browne, 1869, 443.

Small-scale Lumbering Operations

135. Maule, 1938, 42.

136. Maule, 1938, 44.

137. *Homer Mining Index*, June 12, 1880.

138. *Mammoth City Herald*, September 24, 1879.

139. The Porter Mill was located in section 24, T1N/R25E.

140. Maule, 1938, 44.

141. Langille, 1904b, 3.

142. *Mammoth City Herald*, March 23, 1880.

143. *Bodie Chronicle*, April 13, 1880.

144. Billeb, 1957.

145. *Homer Mining Index*, September 11, 1880.

146. Langille, 1904b, 4.

147. *Homer Mining Index*, June 3, 1882.

148. Langille, 1904b, 4; Marshall, 1900, map.

149. *Mammoth City Herald*, May 5, 1880.

150. Maule, 1938, 44.

151. Maule, 1938, 44.

152. *Homer Mining Index*, January 13, 1894.

153. *Homer Mining Index*, May 6 and June 3, 1882.

154. Maule, 1938, 44.

155. Maule, 1938, 44. The Beardsley Sawmill was located in section 7, T1S/R26E. It did not lie in the dry "Sawmill Canyon" shown on the U.S.G.S. "Mono Craters, Ca." topographic quadrangle (15 minute series), but just to the south, on the mapped perennial tributary of Parker Creek.

156. Langille, 1904b, 9.

157. Maule, 1938, 42.

158. Calhoun, 1967, 91.

Agriculture and Grazing

159. Calhoun 1967, 7.

160. Calhoun, 1967, 49.

161. Calhoun, 1967, 45 and map; *Homer Mining Index*, July 1, 1882.

162. Robinson, 1948, 168-171.

163. *Homer Mining Index*, August 7, 1880.

164. *Homer Mining Index*, June 3, 1882.

165. Calhoun, 1967, 23-24.

166. Calhoun, 1967, map.

167. *Homer Mining Index*, May 10, 1884.

168. Harding, 1962, 118.

169. Wasson, 1878, 5-6.

170. Calhoun, 1967, 65.

171. Calhoun, 1967, 48.

172. Maule, 1938, 8; Kersten, 1964, 500.

173. Muir, 1916, 111-112.

174. Russell, 1889, 277-278.

175. Young et al., 1976, 191; Young et al., 1977, 769

176. Calhoun, 1967, 45; *Homer Mining Index*, June 12, 1884.

177. Young et al., 1972, 196.

178. Calhoun, 1967, 40-41.

179. Calhoun, 1967, 38.

180. Langille, 1904a, 38; Busby et al., 1979, 75.

181. Burcham, 1957, 169.

182. Langille, 1904a, 37.

183. Busby et al., 1979, 72; McIntosh, 1908, 45.

184. Langille, 1904a, 38-40.

185. Wasson, 1878, 5-6.

186. Burcham, 1957, 128.

187. Young et al., 1976, 198.

188. The first species to invade the ground laid bare by overgrazing were the broad-leaved annuals Russian thistle (*Salsola*), tansy mustard (*Descurainia*) and filaree (*Erodium*), among others. Following these herbs, once grazing pressures had been somewhat reduced by federal controls, the annual cheat grass (*Bromus tectorum*) moved in as well(Young et al., 1972, 1976).

Post-boom

189. DeGroot, 1890, 336.

190. Leggett, 1894, 419, 434.

191. *Homer Mining Index*, August 4, 1894.

192. Calhoun, 1967, 103.

193. Sampson and Tucker, 1940, 120.

194. McIntosh, 1908, 22.

195. Sampson and Tucker, 1940, 128.

196. Myrick, 1962, 313; Billeb, 1968, 48-50.

POSTSCRIPT

1. Means, 1938, 3-4.

2. The story of this early campaign in the Mono Lake water war--for the war is still being fought today on a much broader front--has never been fully told. For general discussions of the water rights controversy, see: Interagency Task Force on Mono Lake, 1979; Gaines, 1981; and Kahrl, 1982.

LITERATURE CONSULTED

(Newspapers are listed at end)

Aldrich, J. M., 1913. Collecting Notes from the Great Basin and Adjoining Territory. *Entomological News*, 24:214-221.

....., 1921. *Coloradia Pandora* Blake, a Moth of which the Caterpillar is Used as Food by Mono Lake Indians. *Annals*, Entomological Society of America, 14:36-38.

Angel, Myron, ed., 1881. *History of Nevada*. Oakland: Thompson and West.

Bancroft, Hubert Howe, 1885. *History of California*, vol. 3. San Francisco: The History Company.

....., (compiler), undated. *Bancroft Scraps*, vol. 2. California Counties: Los Angeles to Placer. "Mono County," pp. 692-704. At Bancroft Library, University of California, Berkeley.

Barbour, Michael G., and Jack Major, eds., 1977. *Terrestrial Vegetation of California*. New York: John Wiley and Sons.

Bettinger, Robert L., 1982. Archaeology East of the Range of Light: Aboriginal Human Ecology of the Inyo-Mono Region, California. *Monographs in California and Great Basin Anthropology*, No. 1. Davis, California.

Billeb, Emil, 1957. Bodie's Railroad That Was. *Pony Express*, 24(1): 3.

....., 1968. *Mining Camp Days*. Berkeley: Howell-North Books.

Brewer, William H., 1930. *Up and Down California in 1860-1864*. Berkeley: University of California Press. Repr. 1966.

Brockman, C. Frank, 1943. Development of Transportation to Yosemite. *Yosemite Nature Notes*, v. 22, in 3 parts: 22(6): 49-56; 22(7): 57-63; 22(10): 81-86.

Browne, J. Ross, 1868. *The Mineral Resources of the States and Territories West of the Rocky Mountains*. Washington: U. S. Govt. Printing Office.

....., 1869. *Adventures in Apache Country: A Tour Through Arizona and Sonora, with Notes on the Silver Regions of Nevada*. New York: Harper and Brothers.

Buckbee, Edna Bryan, 1935. *The Saga of Old Tuolumne*. New York.

Bunnell, Lafayette Houghton, 1892 (1881). *Discovery of the Yosemite, and the Indian War of 1851 Which Led to that Event*. 3rd ed., revised and corrected. New York: Fleming H. Revell Co.

Burcham, Levi Turner, 1957. *California Range Land: An Historico-ecological Study of the Range Resource of California*. Sacramento: Division of Forestry, Dept. of Natural Resources, State of California.

Busby, Colin I., et al., 1979. *A Culture Resource Overview of the Bureau of Land Management Coleville, Bodie, Benton, and Owens Valley Planning Units, California*. Oakland: Basin Research Associates.

Cain, Ella M., 1956. *The Story of Bodie*. San Francisco: Fearon Publishers.

....., 1961. *The Story of Early Mono County*. San Francisco: Fearon Publishers.

Calhoun, Margaret Currie, 1967. *Pioneers of Mono Basin*. Published by Robert C. Calhoun. Reprinted (1984) by Artemisia Press, Lee Vining.

Chalfant, W. A., 1922 (many later editions). *The Story of Inyo*. Bishop: Published by the author.

....., 1947. *Gold, Guns, and Ghost Towns*. Stanford: Stanford University Press.

Chappell, Maxine, 1947. Early History of Mono County. *Calif. Hist. Soc. Quarterly*, 26: 233-248.

Clark, William B., 1970. Gold Districts of California. Cal. Div. of Mines and Geology *Bulletin*, 193. Sacramento.

Colcord, R. K., 1928. Reminiscences of life in territorial Nevada. *Cal. Hist. Soc. Quarterly*, 7: 112-120.

Crampton, Charles Gregory, 1941. *The Opening of the Mariposa Mining Region, 1848-1859*. Unpublished Ph.D. dissertation, History, University of California, Berkeley.

....., ed., 1957. *The Mariposa Indian War, 1850-1851: The Diaries of Robert Eccleston*. Salt Lake City: Univ. Utah Press.

Davis, Emma Lou, 1962. Hunter-Gatherers of Mono Lake. *The Masterkey*, 36(1): 23-28.

....., 1963. The Desert Culture of the Western Great Basin: A Life-way of Seasonal Transhumance. *AmericanAntiquity*, 29: 202-212.

....., 1964. An Archaeological Survey of the Mono Lake Basin and Excavations of Two Rockshelters, Mono County, California. *Univ. Cal. Arch. Sur. Ann. Rept., 1963-64*, 255-287. Los Angeles.

....., 1965. An Ethnography of the Kuzedika Paiute of Mono Lake, Mono County, California. *Univ. Utah Dept. Anth., Anth. Papers*, 75: 1-55.

Davis, James, 1961. Trade Routes and Economic Exchange Among the Indians of California. *Univ. Cal. Arch. Sur. Report*, no. 54. Berkeley.

DeDecker, Mary, 1966. *Mines of the Eastern Sierra*. Glendale: La Siesta Press.

DeGroot, Henry, 1860. *Sketches of the Washoe Silver Mines, with a Description of the Soil, Climate, and Mineral Resources of the Country East of the Sierras*. San Francisco: Hutchings and Rosenfield.

....., 1890. Mono County. California State Mineralogist, *10th Annual Report*, pp. 336-344.

Dillon, Richard, H., 1965. *J. Ross Browne: Confidential Agent in Old California*. Norman: Univ. Oklahoma Press.

Ernst, Emil F., 1949. An Overlooked Facet of Yosemite History. *Yosemite Nature Notes*, 28(4):25-28.

Ewers, John C., ed., 1959. *Adventures of Zenas Leonard, Fur Trader*. Norman: Univ. Oklahoma Press.

Farquhar, Francis P., 1925. Exploration of the Sierra Nevada, California. *Cal. Hist. Soc. Quarterly*, 4:3-58.

....., 1926. *Place Names of the High Sierra*. San Francisco: Sierra Club.

....., 1928. Lee Vining. *Sierra Club Bulletin*, 13: 83-84.

....., 1943. Jedediah Smith and the First Crossing of the Sierra Nevada. *Sierra Club Bulletin*, 28: 36-53.

....., 1965. *History of the Sierra Nevada*. Berkeley: Univ. Cal. Press.

Gaines, David, 1981. *Mono Lake Guidebook*. Lee Vining: Mono Lake Committee.

Gudde, Erwin G., 1965. *California Place Names*. Berkeley: Univ Cal. Press.

....., 1975. *California Gold Camps.* Edited by Elisabeth K. Gudde. Berkeley: Univ. Cal. Press.

Harding, S. T., 1922. *Report on Development of Water Resources in Mono Basin, Based on Investigations Made for the Division of Engineering and Irrigation.* State Dept. Public Works, Sacramento. Unpublished. On file at Water Resources Center Archives, Univ. Calif., Berkeley.

....., 1962. *Water Supply of Mono Lake Based on its Past Fluctuations.* Unpublished. On file at Water Resources Center Archives, Univ. Calif., Berkeley.

Heizer, Robert F., 1950. Kutsavi, a Great Basin Indian Food. *Kroeber Anth. Soc. Papers,* no. 2: 35-41.

Hoover, Mildred and Hero Rensch, 1966. *Historic Spots in California.* Stanford: Stanford Univ. Press.

Hubbard, Douglass H., 1958. *Ghost Mines of Yosemite.* Fresno: Awani Press.

Interagency Task Force on Mono Lake, 1979. *Report.* Dept. Water Resources, State of California, Sacramento.

Jackson, W. T., 1962. *Historical Material on the Mining Town of Bodie, California: A Critical Bibliography.* Div. Beaches and Parks, Dept. Parks and Recreation, State of California, Sacramento.

Johnson, Russ and Anne, 1967. *The Ghost Town of Bodie as Reported in the Newspapers of the Day.* Bishop: Chalfant Press.

Kahrl, William, 1982. *Water and Power: The Conflict Over Los Angeles Water Supply in the Owens Valley.* Berkeley: Univ. California Press.

Kersten, Earl W., 1964. The Early Settlement of Aurora, Nevada, and Nearby Mining Camps. *Annals,* Association of American Geographers, 54: 490-507.

King, Clarence, 1878. *Report of the U. S. Geological Exploration of the 40th Parallel, Vol. 1: Systematic Geology,* pp. 512-525.

Kroeber, A. L., 1916. California Place Names of Indian Origin. *Univ. Cal. Papers in American Archaeology and Ethnology,* 12: 31-69.

Langille, W. A., 1904a. *Report on the Proposed Owens River Addition to the Sierra Forest Reserve.* Unpublished. Forest Service, U. S. Dept. Agriculture. On file at Forest Service Office, Bishop, California.

....., 1904b. *Township Descriptions of the Lands Examined for the Proposed Owens River Addition to the Sierra Forest Reserve, California.* Unpublished. Bureau of Forestry, U. S. Dept. Agriculture. On file at Forest Service Office, Bishop, Cal.

Lawton, H. W., et al, 1976. Agriculture Among the Paiute of Owens Valley. *Journal of California Anthropology*, 3(1): 13-50.

LeConte, Joseph, 1875. *A Journal of Ramblings Through the High Sierra of California by the University Excursion Party*. San Francisco: The Sierra Club, repr. 1960.

Leggett, Thomas, 1894. Electric Power Transmission Plants and the Use of Electricity in Mining Operations. *Cal. Rept. State Mineralogist*, v. 12, 1892-1894, pp. 413-455.

Leonard, Zenas. *Narrative*. See: Ewers, John C., 1959.

Loeffler, Robert M., 1977. Geology and Hydrology. In Winkler, David, ed., *An Ecological Study of Mono Lake, California*, pp. 6-38. Inst. Ecology Publication no. 12. Davis: Univ. Calif.

Loew, Oscar, 1876. Report on the Alkaline Lakes, Thermal Springs, Mineral Springs, and Brackish Waters of Southern California and Adjacent Country. *Annual Report Upon the Geographical Surveys West of the 100th Meridian*, Appendix H3, pp. 188-199.

Loose, Warren, 1971. *Bodie Bonanza: The True Story of a Flamboyant Past*. New York: Exposition Press.

McIntosh, F. W., compiler, 1908. *Mono County, California: The Land of Promise for the Man of Industry*. Compiled and published by F. W. McIntosh by authority of the Board of Supervisors of Mono County. Reno: Presses of Gazette Publishing Co.

Marshall, R. B., 1900. Mt. Lyell Quadrangle, California. In Gannett, Henry. Classification of Lands. *U. S. Geol. Sur. 21st Annual Report*, 1899-1900, Part V: Forest Reserves. Text, pp. 574-575, and accompanying map.

Maule, William M., 1938. *A Contribution to the Geographic and Economic History of the Carson, Walker, and Mono Basins in Nevada and California*. Calif. Region, Forest Service, U. S. Dept. Agriculture. San Francisco.

Means, Thomas H., 1938. *Report on the Value of Property Sold by the Southern Sierra Power Company and Associated Companies to the City of Los Angeles in 1934 and 1935 Under Contract Dated Oct. 20, 1933*. Unpublished. On file at Water Resources Center Archives, Univ. Calif., Berkeley.

Merriam, C. Hart, 1955. *Studies of California Indians*. Berkeley: Univ. California Press.

Morgan, Dale L., 1953. *Jedediah Smith and the Opening of the West*. Indianapolis: Bobbs-Merrill.

Muir, John, 1911. *My First Summer in the Sierra*. Boston: Houghton Mifflin Co.

....., 1916. *The Mountains of California*. Boston: Houghton Mifflin Co.

Munz, Philip A., and David D. Keck, 1968. *A California Flora*. Berkeley: Univ. Calif. Press.

Myrick, David F., 1962. *Railroads of Nevada and Eastern California. Vol. One: The Northern Roads*. Berkeley: Howell-North Books.

O'Neill, Elizabeth S., 1984. *Meadow in the Sky*. Fresno: Paonorama-West Books.

Parr, J. F., 1928. Reminiscences of the Bodie Strike. *Yosemite Nature Notes*, 7(5): 33-38.

Paul, Rodman, 1947. *California Gold*. Lincoln: Univ. Nebraska Press.

Reimer, George, 1961, *Col. A. W. von Schmidt: His Career as Surveyor and Engineer, 1852-1900*. Unpublished Master's thesis, History, Univ. Calif., Berkeley.

Reveal, Jack L., 1965. Plant Communities of the Mono Basin. In Wahrhaftig, Clyde, et al., eds., *Guidebook for Field Conference I, Northern Great Basin and California*, pp. 104-107. International Assoc. for Quaternary Research (INQUA), 7th Congress.

Robinson, W. W., 1948. *Land in California*. Berkeley: Univ. Calif. Press.

Rundel, Philip W., et al., 1977. Montane and Subalpine Vegetation of the Sierra Nevada and Cascade Ranges. In Barbour, 1977, pp. 559-599.

Russell, Carl Parcher, 1947. *One Hundred Years in Yosemite*. Berkeley: Univ., California Press.

....., 1951. The Geography of the Mariposa Indian War. *Yosemite Nature Notes*, v. 30, in 4 parts: 30(3): 24-30; 30(4): 33-35; 30(6): 52-56; 30(7): 62-71.

Russell, Israel Cook, 1885. Geological History of Lake Lahontan: A Quaternary Lake of Northwestern Nevada. *U.S.G.S. Monographs*, v. XI.

....., 1889. Quaternary History of Mono Valley, California. *U.S.G.S. Eighth Annual Report*, 1886-1887, Part 1, pp. 261-394. Reprinted (1984) by Artemisia Press, Lee Vining

Sampson, R. J. and W. B. Tucker, 1940. Mineral Resources of Mono County. *Calif. Division of Mines Report*, 36: 117-156.

Sanborn, Margaret, 1981. *Yosemite: Its Discovery, Its Wonders, and Its People*. New York: Random House.

Shinn, Charles Howard, 1885. *Mining Camps: A Study in American Frontier Government*. Repr. 1948, Alfred A. Knopf, New York.

Silliman, Benjamin and William Blake, 1864. *Prospectus of the Empire Gold and Silver Mining Company of New York, with Reports thereon of Professor B. Silliman, Jr. of Yale*

College, and of Professor W. P. Blake, Mining Engineer of California. New York: William H. Arthur, Stationer.

Smith, Grant H., 1925. Bodie, the Last of the Old-Time Mining Camps. *Calif. Hist. Soc. Quarterly,* 4: 64-80.

....., 1929. More Notes on Tioga Mining History. *Yosemite Nature Notes,* 8(3): 25-27.

Steward, Julian H., 1933. Ethnography of the Owens Valley Paiute. *Univ. Calif. Publs. in American Archaeology and Ethnology,* 33: 233-350.

Stewart, Omer C., 1941. Culture Element Distributions XIV: Northern Paiute. *Univ. Calif. Anth. Records,* vol. 4, no. 3.

Stine, Scott, 1981. Reinterpretation of the 1857 Surface Elevation of Mono Lake. *Calif. Water Resources Center Rept.* No. 52.

Sullivan, Maurice, 1934. *The Travels of Jedediah Smith.* Santa Ana, Calif.: Fine Arts Press.

Thomas, Benjamin E., 1952. The California-Nevada Boundary. *Annals,* Assoc. Amer. Geog., 42(1): 51-68.

Trexler, Keith A., 1961. *The Tioga Road: A History, 1883-1961.* Yosemite Natural History Association.

Twain, Mark, 1972 (1872). *Roughing It.* Berkeley: Univ. Calif. Press.

Vasek, Frank, and Robert F. Thorne, 1977. Transmontane Coniferous Vegetation. In Barbour, 1977, pp. 797-832.

Von Schmidt, A. W., 1855. *Field Notes of the Extension* [of the Mt. Diablo Baseline, California]. Book 104-3. Deposited at the Office of the Bureau of Land Management, Sacramento, Calif.

....., [1856]. *Personal Notebook,* inscribed on endpaper "Book No. 2." In the Bancroft Library, Univ. of Calif., Berkeley, among Mott-Von Schmidt Family Papers.

Wasson, Joseph, 1878. *Bodie and Esmeralda: An Account of the Important Revival of Mining Interests in the Bodie and Esmeralda Districts.* San Francisco: Spaulding, Barto and Co.

....., 1879. *Complete Guide to the Mono County Mines: A Description of Bodie, Esmeralda, Indian, Lake, Laurel Hill, Prescott, and Other Mining Districts.* San Francisco: Spaulding, Barto and Co.

Watson, Douglas, 1934. *West Wind: The Life of Joseph Reddeford Walker.* Los Angeles: privately printed.

Wedertz, Frank, 1969. *Bodie: 1859-1900*. Bishop: Chalfant Press.

....., 1978. *Mono Diggings*. Bishop: Chalfant Press.

Wheat, Carl Irving, 1942. *The Maps of the California Gold Region*. San Francisco: Grabhorn Press.

....., 1957. *Mapping the Trans-Mississippi West*. San Francisco: The Institute of Historical Cartography.

Whiting, H. A., 1888. Mono County. *Calif. State Mineralogist, 8th Annual Report*, pp. 352-401. Sacramento.

Whitney, Josiah Dwight, 1865. *Geological Survey of California, Vol. 1: Geology*, pp. 540-542.

Young, James A., et al., 1972. Alien Plants in the Great Basin. *Jour. Range Management*, 25: 194-201.

....., 1976. Great Basin Plant Communities, Pristine and Grazed. *Nevada Arch. Sur. Research Paper*, 6: 187-215.

....., 1977. Sagebrush Steppe. In Barbour, 1977, pp. 763-796.

Newspapers

(All are on microfilm at the Bancroft Library, University of California, Berkeley.)

On Bodie and Mono Basin:

Homer Mining Index, Lundy California. Broken file, June 12, 1880 to Oct. 1, 1884. Renewed publication in 1894; broken file for that year.

Mammoth City Herald, Mammoth City, California. Broken file, July 1879 to February 1881.

Bodie Weekly Standard-News, Bodie, California. Title varies: *Bodie Standard, Bodie Weekly Standard, Weekly Bodie Standard, Bodie Standard Weekly.* Broken file from Nov. 1877 to Aug. 1882.

Mono Alpine Chronicle, Bodie, California (part of *Bridgeport Chronicle Union* file). Published at Bodie from Dec. 1878 to Oct. 1880.

Bodie Daily Free Press, Bodie California. Broken file, Nov. 1879 to Jan. 1884.

Daily Bodie Standard, Bodie, California. Broken file from Dec. 1878 to July, 1880.

On Tredwell Moore's 1852 Expedition:

Stockton Journal, Stockton, California. Aug. 24, 1852.

Alta California, San Francisco, California. July 15 and August 26, 1852.

San Francisco Herald, San Francisco, California. August 26 and 28, 1852.

On Von Schmidt's 1855 Survey:

Sacramento Daily Union, Sacramento, California. Aug. 8, 1855.